If You See Kay

by

Wendel Agne

PublishAmerica
Baltimore

First printing

ISBN: 1-4137-9673-7
PUBLISHED BY PUBLISHAMERICA, LLLP
www.publishamerica.com
Baltimore

Printed in the United States of America

Chapter I

I've had me many a magic day
bedding a lovely maid.
But tell her, please, if you see Kay,
she was the best I've laid.

*B*RAD thought of that doggerel on the drive back to Newark airport and grinned at the remembered high school pun. But that was later. Now he was driving the rented car toward Kay, testing, as he used to in high school, how fast he could speed through the toll booth and still throw quarters into the basket. Best shot—twenty-three mph. He wondered how much the attendant made picking up missed coins. That triggered a memory of the teen-aged times, back about 1940, taking the toll road on his motorcycle to the Jersey shore when he was short of money. At the toll booth, his pal would pop off the buddy seat, scoop up missed coins, and they reached the shore with enough funds for fun. But now every third thought was, of course, about Kay.

He had known her for seventeen years, since he was twelve. So many memories passed through his mind. Mostly, he focused on his last visit, two years ago, returning from teaching a year in France (ah France! le beau pays!) He phoned, she was thrilled, he arrived late in the morning. The long, luxurious path past well-tended lawns and flowers up to the pillared, wrap-around porch, the bay windows, the wrought-iron filigree on the Mansard roof of the spacious home—all bespoke the wealth of Kay's father, who lived in the Wall Street world in New York and maintained this place (which he seldom visited) for his wife, his son, his daughter, her husband and her child. It had been a second home for Brad. There was a simple explanation why he was so close to this woman who was twenty-five when he was twelve. Her brother, Dexter T. Wainscott IV, Brad's age, came down from Hilltop Terrace to the playground and they became close friends.

Driving along, Brad remembered how her mother, who had never warmed to him, answered the door, took his arm and escorted him to the back porch, talking continuously so as not to give him a chance to ask about Kay. The mother had alerted Dex that Brad was coming, hoping Dex would arrive before Brad could get to Kay.

But soon Kay appeared in the doorway, wearing a chiffon nightgown, a lacy robe, high-heeled slippers (she always wore high heels), and her usual teasing, friendly smile. "Are you coming *up?*" she asked while turning and leaving. He watched her walk through the living room, into the hall and up the stairs. Calling someone a "horse's ass" is a strange insult. A horse walking away is a beautiful motion—high hips gently swaying, limbs moving so smoothly that the slightly turned-out feet seemed to be heading back up as they touched the ground. Kay walked like that.

She was slender in all the right —tiny high-arched feet, ankles, back, clavicles, neck, arms, fingers; and amply soft in the other right places—thighs, breasts and buttocks. Her face was not pretty but always enticingly lively. Her nose turned up too much and her front buck teeth slightly overlapped.

However, this gave a kissing look to her upper lip which

always drew Brad's eyes. Her eyes always looked as if they had a delicious secret to tell.

There was nothing strange about Kay being in bed in the middle of the day. She often was "not feeling well." While she honestly told herself that, there was a deeper reason why daytime often found her in bed. She derived enormous pleasure from the relaxed position, the feel of flimsy clothing, the snuggly covers, the intimacy with oneself. She read voraciously, eclectically, and vicariously in bed. Childhood illness and some minor operations showed her that bed meant special attention. Her first sexual experience, at the age of twelve, was while lying in a hospital bed. Dr. Lude had just finished examining every inch of her—a few places by the half inch. She was panting heavily. He placed her hand on his pants and said, "This is too big for you now, but when you get bigger, we'll have great fun with it." And they did. Whenever she thought of bed, it was never about sleeping, but what a wonderful place it was for being awake.

Brad said to the mother, "I'd better go up or she'll think I don't want to see her," while racing from the room without giving mother a chance to answer.

As he entered her bedroom, she teased, "You seem to prefer my mother to me." Before she could finish, he was already kissing her and caressing his way along her leg and body toward her breast.

"My hand is at home again," he said. "Every part of me missed you so, while I was in France."

"Some parts more than others?" she asked.

"No, really," he insisted, "I missed you all over. My toes wanted your toes."

"Hmmmmm," she drawled her delicious drawl.

"And I longed to hear that hmmmmm," he whispered, kissing her again. "Oh God," he moaned, "I've got to have you right now!"

"Brad, any moment Dex will come charging through that

door, and all three of us would be very embarrassed. Tomorrow we're going to the shore for a month. I'll invite you to come down Thursday. You come down Wednesday and get a motel room. I'll meet you there Wednesday evening."

"Wonderful! But now?"

"You know we can't."

"Yes, yes, yes! You stand by the door with the door slightly open, so you can see if Dex is coming." And so his hard, hairy abdomen pressed against her soft, smooth buttocks, his fingers caressed her nipples and massaged her clitoris. The Love Goddess kept Dex away long enough for desire to be fulfilled, and they came before he did.

At the motel, for the first time in this fourteen-year-long affair, they made love leisurely and in perfect privacy. During his three-day stay at their cottage, Dex and Brad renewed adolescent summers, riding the waves, playing catch on the beach, shooting wooden ducks at the amusement park and crabbing in Barnagat Bay. Crabbing was enjoyable frustration. You attached a weight to a string. A few inches above the weight, you fastened a fish head. You lowered the string in the bay until the weight hit the bottom. You raised it a bit and waited until you felt a crab tugging. Slowly and smoothly, you pulled up the string so the poor dumb crab did not realize that eating would change to eaten. When he was about a foot from the surface, you swiftly scooped your net under him and brought up—a weight and a half-eaten fish head.

Despite mothers and brothers and husbands and children, Kay and Brad made love under the boardwalk, in the ocean on a sandbar, in a rowboat, behind a store, high up in a Ferris wheel, and straddling a toilet in a locked bathroom.

As he now drove toward her, he relived every instant of that last visit, every detail as clear as if he were watching a movie. Then his attention turned back to how it all started.

Chapter II

*B*ACK in the '30s, a "big kid" meant short and fat or tall and skinny. Brad was an exception. By the age of ten, he was only slightly taller than the other boys, but was built like a mature athlete. When he arrived at a summer camp for boys ten to twelve, the other kids started asking him questions—what's the food like, when do we swim, are there rattlesnakes. Brad said, "Why are you asking me? I just got here, like you."

They all laughed and said, "Come on, we know you're our counselor."

Brad protested, "I'm eleven years old, I'm one of you guys." They laughed louder and only stopped when the real counselor arrived. In elementary school, he thought he scored ten touchdowns per game because of his tremendous talent. In truth, he dodged some and outran some, but mostly ran over those helpless, puny children. By twelve, he was five feet eight inches and 170 pounds, all muscle. He looked at least sixteen years old. His father stupidly let him drive when they were together and for fun would stop and ask a cop for directions. Dexter had come down to the town playground and was watching kids bounce off Brad on his way to the end zone. After the game, Dex went up to Brad and said, "Wow!

You're really good!"

Trying to appear modest, Brad replied, "Their team was pretty bad. Our team is much better. You're new here, right? Just moved in?"

"No, I don't get down here much. I've lived on Hilltop Terrace for a long time. I go to Prescott Academy." Hilltop Terrace and Prescott Academy were in Brad's town, but were worlds away from his apartment-house neighborhood.

Brad had never been inside any of the large houses up there and eagerly agreed to go home with Dex for lunch. He tried not to be in awe of the place, the rugs, the furniture, the art works. Dexter's sister, Kay, put him at ease with her ready laugh, and joked that he was lying about his age so he wouldn't have to go to work. She made them sandwiches of peanut butter, bacon, lettuce and mayonnaise on some strange, wonderful bread. Brad asked if they ate unusual stuff all the time.

"Of course," Kay answered, "tonight we're having chocolate soup, broiled zebra tails, grasshopper salade, and eggplant pudding." And they all laughed.

Dexter was anxious to get Brad into the poolroom so he could show off his own talent. But Brad kept engaging Kay in conversation. "Dex said you have a three-year-old kid. Where is she?"

"Out back with my mother. Grandparents play with their grandchildren better than parents do. I take care of the feeding, clothing and daily tantrums."

Dex jumped in, "I have this great football board game, I use book matches for players, because the match heads look like helmets, and I collect all different colors. Like, I have matches with orange heads and black stems for Princeton. Sometimes I sprinkle salt on the board so we're playing in snow."

Turning back to Kay, Brad asked, "Do you play games with Dex?"

"Well, I often try to make believe we're not thirteen years

apart. We play Monopoly and pick-up sticks, but I am much older with no siblings in between. We're very happy to have Dex. Still, my parents thought that I was the end. You know, the Pennsylvania Railroad doesn't always pull out on time."

Brad was a little shocked and very pleased that she spoke so freely with him. It was the first time ever he felt on equal footing with a "woman."

Dex eventually got Brad to shoot pool, see his bubblegum baseball card collection, and roll the dice for the Princeton-Dartmouth football game in the snow. These games were not played in silence. Whoever had the ball got to be the radio announcer—"and here comes Luke the Spook into the game, wearing number 28, the same number worn eight years ago by the great Goose Johnson. He slashes off tackle for twelve yards!"

The board said only "gains 12."Actually, this merely imitated real baseball announcers on the radio. Stations did not want to pay for an announcer going to an away game, so he would stay in the studio and receive a ticker-tape message: Dimaggio flies out. He would say, "Joltin' Joe rubs some dirt on his bat, steps into an outside curve and sends it deep into left field. His brother, Dom, makes a nice running catch. So much for family friendship, right?"

Yet the feeling of Kay's presence in the house never left Brad. So it was with his almost daily visits. Dex and Brad became best friends. Kay and Brad became even closer. They began touching in innocent ways—a hand on a shoulder, an "ah go on" push, a hold to prove how strong he was, a four-hands greeting that lasted very long. Brad loved to sing and she played the piano well enough to get through popular songs. When he sang "You'll never know just how much I love you," he knew that she did know how much and she knew he knew.

The inevitable day arrived. Kay's mother had taken her grandchild to the park. The husband, as always, was at work.

Dexter was at Prescott Academy. Brad's school was closed for teachers' conferences. At 10:00 AM, he rang Kay's bell. She had been reading in bed and answered the bell in her satin pajamas and satin robe. She took his arm with both of her hands and escorted him to the couch. "What a surprise! But really, when you play hooky, you should do something exciting, not visit an old lady."

"You're a young lady and very exciting ."

"You know, you're quite good with words. You should try writing."

"I have. I've written this poem for you," he said handing her the following:

> the sun might hide behind a cloud,
> the cynic's songs are sung out loud,
> the darkest darkness of the night
> can fill the shepherd's flock with fright
> But nothing natural or made
> by man can make me be afraid,
> or even feel a little blue,
> when I am near this perfect you.

"That's very nice. I'm deeply flattered. And good writing," she said, kindly not adding "for a twelve-year-old."

She sat on a small love seat, expecting him to sit in a nearby chair. Instead, he squeezed in next to her, very aware that their knees were touching. She laughed and said, "Don't you feel squashed?"

"No," he answered, "I want to be close to you."

A huge conflict raged within him. He passionately yearned to kiss her. He panicked in fear to kiss her. What would she do? Scream? Hit him? Call his father? He kissed her. Her smile was half motherly, half girlfriend. He kissed her again. And again. They weren't actually what any adult lover would call kisses. His hands remained grasping his own thighs. He puckered his lips tight, took dead aim at her mouth, hit the target and recoiled, like throwing a tennis ball against a wall.

Still mostly motherly, Kay asked, "Shall I teach you how to kiss?"

"Oh yes," he pleaded.

She placed one of his arms over her shoulder and the other around her waist. He felt the bones of her slender back. "Kissing isn't like crunching crackers. It's like letting ice cream melt in your mouth. It's like sinking your fingers into the soft fur of a cat. Let your lips roam slowly over mine." And he did. It was totally different than all the little girls he had ever kissed and totally thrilling. Without her realizing it, the mother mode vanished and lust engulfed her. She felt his young, lean muscles and both of them trembled with desire. His hand around her waist slowly moved forward along her ribs, and she ached to have it reach her breast.

"Do you want me to?" he asked. The question jolted her, because she suddenly realized he was not being timid or polite. He was asking if she was a lady or a whore, and he desperately, despite his passion, wanted her to be a lady. Good god, she thought, I almost seduced this child!

She jumped up and said frivolously, "Lesson's over! You're a very fast learner! Now go play football." And she rushed him out the door with a motherly kiss before he could protest.

Ah, how seldom things are ended when they are ended. While Kay allowed, after that, short hugs and few kisses, they touched a lot and held hands, even in public, even when her husband was present, although that fellow was seldom present, as he and his secretary had so much work to do. Kay grew fond of Brad, and he worshiped her every movement and every word.

In those days, before television, radio played the same role. Dexter and Brad would argue about who was the greatest hero: *Buck Rogers in the 25th Century*! or "Jack Armstrong, the all-American boy, is on the air!" or "With a cloud of dust and the speed of light and a hearty 'Hiyo, Silver,' the Lone Ranger!" Once a week, late at night, was *The Witch's Tale*. A raspy old lady's voice would say, "Well, Satan," (her meowing cat) "what sweet little bedtime story do we have for the kiddies tonight?" and proceed with some gruesome horror about a detached hand stalking the guy who chopped it off. It was a weekly ritual that Brad would listen to these bloody tales with his second family in the pitch dark with only the faint glow of the radio in a distant corner. On one such night, the husband was, as always, away on "business," the mother felt too tired to stay up, Dex attended a special event at his academy, and Kay and Brad sat on the sofa, shaking from the radio's screams. Their thighs were touching and they held hands on Brad's thigh. He became intensely aware of how close her hand was to his hard longing. Uncontrollably, he moved her hand to it and wrapped her fingers around it. She did not move her hand away. He reached over and pressed her lap, feeling the hard pelvic bone. She seemed to be pushing his hand away, until he realized she had pushed his hand to the bottom of her skirt. He felt the soft thigh beneath her silk stocking, then the even softer flesh above the stocking. He searched her abdomen in vain for her opening. Finally, to his amazement, his hand found what it was frantically looking for way down between her legs. All this while, their mouths engulfed each other's. Kay directed his hand to massage her clitoris as she unclothed his penis, pulling his long foreskin back and forth over the head. Their moans were augmented by the groans and shrieks from the radio. The panting and gasping quickened and they came. Brad curled up in a trembling ball. She combed her fingers through his hair.

Dexter dashed in through the door, yelling "Is *The Witch's Tale* still on?"

"Yes," Kay answered with a devilish smile, "but you missed the climax."

For the next two weeks, one question kept tormenting Brad: When would they be safely and completely alone long enough to make love. He had to be satisfied with many brief moments when the longed-for aroma lingered on his finger or his lips tasted her erect nipples. Finally came the evening of Mother's Day. Dex took his mother to a movie. The husband's only presence was flowers sent from far away. Kay greeted Brad wearing satin pajamas. He rushed her to the bedroom, pulled her pants down around her ankles, unzipped his fly and was about to enter when she lost patience.

"Either take my pants off or pull them back up!" He almost died.

"I'm sorry, I'm sorry, I'm sorry," he pleaded, almost crying, as he rushed down to her feet and removed the offending pants. Kissing her legs, he kept pleading, "I'm sorry, I'm sorry." As his lips reached the top of her thigh, she hoped his tongue was heading for that excitable little bump, but his only thought was to be inside of her, and immediately he was. Because of an exceptionally long foreskin, which was smooth and moist on the inside, he knew from masturbating the simple sexual thrill. It was closer to the real thing than he thought it would be, but it was, of course, nothing like the real thing.

None of the three men who had ever been inside her had moved so fast and furiously. Faster and faster. His corduroy pants felt strange and harsh against her thighs. With a cry of pain, he collapsed on her. She gave him time to recover and got up. She removed her top. For the first time, Brad gazed on all of her. Nothing had ever seemed so beautiful to him. With her usual bemused smile, she said, "Now that the intense hunger is satisfied, we can enjoy the feast." She undressed him, and he tasted all the delicious dishes he never imagined existed.

Chapter III

*B*ECAUSE Dexter and Brad were best friends, the lovers could go places together, Kay accompanying the boys as the responsible adult. Amusement parks, ball games, swimming pools, movies, picnics—all afforded opportunities to enjoy each other and sneak in their affair. The circumstances were just difficult enough to maintain a frustrating edge, which heightened the longing. The boy enjoyed feeling like a man, and the woman enjoyed feeling like a girl again. Their very different other lives went on.

Brad's family were of German heritage and right-wing Republicans. His father would read the newspapers and listen to radio commentators mainly to rant against their liberal nonsense. He even told Brad that President Roosevelt was Jewish, having changed his name from Rosenfeld. He apparently was unaware of Teddy Roosevelt's relation. He called the Vice-President "Hairy Ass Truman."

A relative, Dr. Lars T. Bradenhoff, had brought Brad out into this world, thus Brad's name. This gentleman, with a handlebar mustache, who exercised bare-chested with dumbbells in his backyard, even in the snow, while little Brad watched from a window, was known as "Uncle Lars." Now Brad's father euphemistically used "arse" for "ass," as in "he's a pain in the arse." So little Brad, not knowing how the good doctor spelled his name, did not hear two L sounds and thought his name was "Uncle Arse," which sent him giggling whenever he addressed him, much puzzling this solemn man.

Brad lived with his father, spending a day every week or two with his mother. His siblings, all much older, were either married or living with their mother. Brad lived with his father because, after the divorce, his mother was absorbed with her new life, and the father doted on his four-year-old son. One blizzardy night at 3:00 AM, the mother called the father, saying the desperately lonely child had been screaming all day and night, "I want my daddy!" Cars could not move, so the father trudged through the snow for two miles. He pulled the child back to his apartment on a sled. The child grinned all the way, looking up at his daddy's back, a big, strong back which had rescued him from the dragon's den and was taking him home through this treacherous mountain pass. Let's not mention that the father was following the trolley tracks.

Brad's mother was raised with tutors on a Long Island country estate. At sixteen, her father died. At eighteen, to escape a cruel and lecherous step-father, she eloped with Brad's father, a poor but charming local young man. When her mother died a few years later, she inherited the estate, with its large house, its own private little lake, and a half mile of Long Island Sound beach. They had three children there, one of whom fell through the ice and was never seen again. Almost at the same time, a firebug maid burned down the house, and Brad's mother was fed up with country living. She sold the estate and they moved to NYC. Then, when the money was gone from very bad investments, they moved across the Hudson to Newark. Allies of Brad's mother blamed the father. Allies of the father said that he felt it was her money, so he butted out. The truth is they were both guilty.

This all happened long before Brad accidentally arrived when she was forty-three.

After thirty-two years of cooking and cleaning and changing diapers, she decided this was her time—hers and her talent. In what little spare time she had as a housewife, she wrote dozens of pop songs—dreamy love songs about Hawaii, sad "lover, lover, where have you gone" songs in the minor key, silly "Arty chokes on artichokes" songs, and songs on every imaginable ethnic, geographic, seasonal and workplace topic. She'd send them to publishers, who sent them back. So her plan was to get a divorce and hit the nightclub circuit, turning her novelty songs into skits, hoping that some mogul would catch her act and either she or her songs would hit it big. Her husband thought she had gone crazy. Her older children were deeply embarrassed. Brad was entranced. When he visited her, she would rehearse for him, and they would sing her songs together. She got gigs in little, local nightclubs for very little money. It was the last days of silent movies. She got a job playing the piano to accompany the soundless films. When the small boy went to the movie house with her, he was so proud that all these people paid money to sit in the dark to listen to his mother play. Although he did find it strange that they kept staring at a square, lighted area. Even she watched it while playing.

Sometimes she would take little Brad to visit relatives for a weekend. Long Island was rural in the late 1920s. To Brad it felt like a foreign country. He had never before seen an outhouse nor an icebox. His ten-year-old cousin took him rabbit hunting with a real rifle. His eyes and mouth sprang open as he watched Aunt Fran procure dinner by walking out into the yard, grabbing a chicken by the head and whipping its body in the air, breaking its neck. Brad skipped the meat that night.

Her stage career lasted six years, till Brad was ten. She dressed like Sherlock Holmes for her song, "I Need Clues for

My Blues to Catch You." She dressed like a hermaphrodite and sang "I'm in Love With the Other Half of Me." She dressed like a clown for "Don't Laugh at My Love."

She died a slow, horrible death of abdominal cancer. Brad was at her bedside on her last day. She asked him to sing the song she had written for him. Somehow, he managed to get through "My Little Son, When Your Life Was Begun, Then Heaven Smiled on Me." A few hours later she was dead. That night he suddenly felt guilty about an event that happened a year earlier. A big hit radio program was "Major Bowles Amateur Hour." The contestants came in all varieties, but they particularly liked kids. Brad's father knew someone who got him an audition. He sang the number-one song on the "Hit Parade"—"Never In a Million Years." Brad had a nice voice, but not one for big-time radio. He got turned down. When he told his mother about the audition, she was warm and loving, as always, and rehearsed him. He remembered contemplating singing one of her songs, and felt she was hoping he would. Even though he was only ten now, and only nine then, he felt selfish and mean. Ironically, what he did not realize, was that the mother-son gimmick probably would have considerably enhanced his chances.

Missing on the radio show did not gravely disappoint him. The only singing sorrow that stayed with him happened in the eighth grade. Every Christmas, five eighth-grade boys were chosen to sing the five verses of "We Three Kings." For eight years, he yearned to be one of them. When the time came, they chose him first! He had his pick and chose the dark stanza, "Myrrh is mine, its bitter perfume, breathes a life of gathering gloom. Sorrowing, sighing, bleeding, dying, sealed in a cold, stone tomb." When the assembly day arrived, he had such a sore throat that he could not talk, much less sing.

Brad's father had worked his way up from office boy to an undercover investigator for the Pinkerton Detective Agency. As a born liar, he fell perfectly into the job. By the time Brad came along, he was a supervisor. No longer having the professional opportunity for subterfuges, he practiced them in his private life. The truth pained him. It seemed so dull. If he was home, Brad should say he went to the store. If he went to the store, Brad should say he was picking someone up at the airport. Lying for him was not a deception. It was an art form. Brad loved his father's wild tales about his younger days, when he ran down three flights with bullets whizzing past him. This happened when he was with a suspect from a jewel robbery in a third-floor walk-up. The father never carried a gun, claiming it made him look more innocent when frisked. But this guy seemed to be onto him, as he told Brad's father to notice the bullet holes in the wall behind his chair. The father laughed and said, "I bet his last thought was 'This chair is so comfortable, I could sit here forever.'" And he laughed again, and asked, "Mind if I have a drink?" "Help yourself." The father walked over to the table, filled a glass with gin, threw it in the crook's eyes and flew down the stairs.

Another time, his father jumped off a freight train as a bum to join a hobo gang to find out who was stealing coal. He wasn't afraid the bums would give him a beating, but would give him a disease, because they brewed coffee in a big can, which they passed around. Everyone took one sip. They watched your Adam's apple to make sure you took only one sip. The can went round and round. He couldn't dare refuse to put his lips where theirs had been.

One job involved a dentist who lost two fingers when a taxi driver slammed a door on his hand. He collected a fortune for being unable to work. The dentist was helping his nephew take over the practice. Brad's dad persuaded the dentist to extract a tooth, thus extracting the fortune from the dentist.

Then there was the woman whose accident supposedly confined her to a wheelchair, living it up in Atlantic City on insurance money. Brad's dad wooed her and got her to dance in her hotel room.

These stories were actually true, and so good that they didn't need embellishing. Even as a supervisor, he thrilled his son one weekend by bringing home a suitcase full of guns, evidence for a Monday trial. The kid covered himself with them.

The joy of life gushed out of him. He'd rush in and scoop up Brad to see a fire or an accident or a sunset or a hailstorm. He was out a lot, playing cards, shuffleboard in a bar, bowling, shooting pool, and always took Brad with him. Brad could play poker before he could read. The father felt very disappointed when Brad spent so much time with Dexter's family, not knowing it was to be near Kay. Although he never hit Brad, he was as quick to rage as he was to laughter, particularly road rage. Many a time Brad cringed in the passenger seat while his dad challenged some gigantic truck driver.

Once Kay took Brad, his father and Dex to a play. (Unconsciously, she was always educating Brad, as she shared with him her voracious reading—in bed, of course—of the "best" authors.) The play was *Native Son*, and the producer/director, Orson Welles, had insisted that Negroes be allowed in the audience. Brad's father went along only because he was sure there would be a race riot, and he didn't want to miss the action. By the third act, when nothing but the play had happened, he was sound asleep. At this point in the play, Bigger Thomas is cornered in a railroad shack. Welles had "police" planted in the audience, shouting, "Come out, you black bastard !" and shooting guns. Brad's father popped up with glee. "See! I told you! Let's get out of here!" and tried to drag his crew out while they tried pulling him back into his seat.

Brad finished the eighth grade unaware that he had a genuine gift for language, not caring that he got average grades when he could have been an excellent student. His teacher was stunned when, after the class had read "Casey at the Bat," Brad handed in his football version of it, "O'Grady of Mudville":

> The ball rested smack on the fifty,
> the clock said ten seconds to play.
> The score was tied seven to seven,
> a touch would save Mudville the day.
> Into the game came O'Grady!
> No longer could wounds keep him out.
> So fast was he, even on one foot he could have played with the gout!
> The ball went straight back to O'Grady. He spun as he faked to the half.
> The fake fooled the defense so deftly that even their coach had to laugh.
> 100 times 100 people watched yardlines pass under his feet!
> 10,000 delirious people watched paydirt and O'Grady meet!
> Now the moral of this story's as follows: though strive for perfection always,
> a person must have one exception, one error, at least, in his days.
> The crowd that day cared not for morals, they only wished to shame and blame
> O'Grady, once idol, now villain, for his safety cost Mudville the game.

The next week, the teacher assigned the writing of a sonnet, with the first line "Today I saw her on a crowded street." Brad wrote:

> Today I saw her on a crowded street,
> the girl I'd seen only in dreams before,
> the girl I'd always worship and adore

and build a pedestal beneath her feet.
I had to inch up close, yet be discreet.
The fragrance of her perfume filled the air.
Solidified my dream became so sweet.
Of nothing else but her was I aware.
Yet minor details dreams have always banned.
They are just beauteous visions in a blur.
Ah now, I saw so clearly all of her—
her face, her walk, her slender grace, her hand.
And so in dreams I failed to see the thing
which kept me from my love—a plain gold ring.

This was, of course, inspired by Kay's wedding ring. The class had also recently read Keats' "On first looking into Chapman's Homer," where the author feels the amazement of the explorer's first view of the Pacific Ocean, "silent on a peak at Darien." Maryanne Chaplin was a girl in Brad's class. Along with the sonnet, Brad handed in this:

On first looking into Chaplin's homework

Much have I stumbled in the realms of books,
and many Math problems left unsolved.
My many vows to study unresolved
and rightly earned my teacher's dirty looks.

Yet never knew a girl could be so bright
till Chaplin's homework swam into my ken.
I would not have to work at all tonight!
Because I took a peek at Maryanne's!

This eighth grader so impressed the teacher that she stopped him in the hall and said, "Brad, do you know that you can become a fine poet?" He was stunned and not flattered. A POET!? Aren't they frail, consumptive sissies? He hoped writing poetry wouldn't turn him into a poet.

All summer long, he thought only of high school football, aside from Kay. There would be one year of junior varsity, then three glorious varsity years. All summer long, he worked out and practiced jukes which would get him into the end zone. Only a driving rain kept him indoors, reading joke books with Dexter. Each would have a different edition of *A Thousand and One Jokes*. They would sit glum faced, turning pages. Then every few minutes one of them would burst out laughing and share the joke—"The butcher backed into the meat grinder and got a little behind in his work" or "Meet me in front of the pawn shop and I'll kiss you under the balls."

Of course, there was the Fourth of July. As soon as the school year ended in late June, Brad and his friends anticipated the Fourth, not with patriotic fervor, but with a chance to blow up the neighborhood. Out of town, vacant fields were covered with huge temporary tents, in which you could buy every conceivable type of firecracker: little "lady fingers" strung together to go off in rapid succession, like a machine gun; "torpedoes" which exploded when you threw them against a wall or high up to crash down on the street, preferably near a girl; "cherry bombs," named from their appearance, powerful enough to blast a tin can twenty feet in the air. Kids set up toy villages and bombarded them to smithereens. Brad was walking up and down the aisles of the tent, carefully using his allotted money, when he froze in awe, staring at the largest firecracker he had ever seen. It stood nine inches tall with a three-inch diameter. He pictured buildings collapsing for miles around. It cost half of his total allowance, but how could he resist? The Fourth arrived, and the Great Destroyer was placed in the middle of a large yard and given an extra-long fuse. The gang stood far back in delight and terror. The fuse was lit! The Great Destroyer made a muffled "poof" as it shot something up fifteen feet in the air, and down came a little American flag on a little parachute. Patriotism had conquered barbarism after all.

The summer ended. A week before school started, the call went out for freshman football tryouts. To Brad's amazement and horror, 170 kids showed up! They lined up and the coach shouted, "Now I know this is going to sound cruel and unfair, but the fact is, I can only work with about fifty of you, and I have to make that cut right here and now." *Oh my God,* thought Brad, *we're going to draw straws! He doesn't know how good I am, and the odds are against me!* "Now," the coach continued, "Roll up your pants as far as you can, take off your shirts, put your arms up and make a muscle." A big grin widened Brad's mouth. Very few boys could match his muscles.

Brad and the others selected went to the locker room for uniforms. An hour later, they were back in line, looking like football players. The coach placed a football on the ground. "Anybody think they know how to center the ball?" (In those days, the center really passed the ball, leading the runner the way the quarterback leads a wideout today.) A stocky kid jumped forward and stood over the ball. The coach walked up and down the line, looking the boys over. "You," to Brad, "go stand next to him." *Wow,* thought Brad, *I was the first one chosen!* As the choosing continued and a formation developed, it suddenly hit Brad—*I'm a guard! A guard? A guard! What in the hell does a guard do? What does he guard?* In elementary school, he saw his linemen in front of him and he heard they did something called "blocking," but he had just run over them as well as the opponents. Now he was supposed to seek out the enemy and bump into them. Even worse, he was supposed to find one particular guy and bump into him. For two weeks, he tried and felt lost, although the coach seemed satisfied. Then it burst out of him—"Coach, I'm a real good ball carrier, really real good. Gimme a shot." The coach laughed loudly and started to walk away. But he liked Brad's spirit and turned back.

Still laughing, he asked, "Really real good?"

"Gimmme a shot," Brad repeated.

"Tell you what," the coach said, grinning, "for today's practice, you're a half-back. If you're not great—I mean great—back to guard and ten laps for wasting my time."

God, it felt good to stand behind the center, anticipating the snap, catching the ball, tucking it under his arm. He leaped toward the hole. It closed. He spun and streaked around the end. He put a move on the linebacker and broke up the middle. He was juking the safety when the cornerback came up behind him. A shoulder pad rammed into the side of his knee, arms grabbed his foot and twisted on the way down. Then an excruciating pain. The next thing he remembered was lying on the training table in the locker room, with the knee still hurting almost as much as the first jolt. The coach put his hand on Brad's head and said, "I'll cancel the ten laps, and when your knee gets better, I'll give you another shot."

But the knee did not get better. He was on crutches for three weeks, a cane for three weeks, limped another month, and when he tried light jogging, the pain and swelling returned. He spent the season watching from the bench. Knee surgery was lousy in the '30s, and the operation left him worse than before. Eventually, only a slight limp remained, and he could even run if no one bumped his knee, but his football days had ended.

He did not realize this was a multiple blessing. First of all, it preserved his teeth—they did not wear face masks back then. One sensible parent insisted that her son wear a face mask. You can imagine what the poor boy went through. They would be running laps, and some kid would shout, "Stop! Nobody move! Carl forgot his face mask!"

More valuable than saving teeth, the extra time saved his brain, turning his attention to many more important things.

He actually thought about things brought up in school—history, politics, characters and ideas in literature. Strangest of all, he thought about Jesus and this Christian religion he was born into. The Bible's portrait of Jesus startled and disturbed him. Jesus seemed so out of sync with so many Old Testament quotations he kept hearing from Christians. Brad loved the Old Testament stories of love and war and treachery, but he wondered why they were in the Christian Bible. The Jewish God was so different than the God of Jesus.

His family had never been overtly religious, never said grace except on Thanksgiving. He never went to Sunday school. When the minister said to the crowded Christmas congregation, "Well, I'll see you all on Easter," he meant Brad's family. Recently, because he enjoyed singing, he joined the church choir. So every Sunday, he heard a sermon from this intelligent, well-read, deep-thinking minister. Although Brad did not know the word "metaphysics," that's what he yearned for. Football had been a perfectly orderly world, clearly defining how you scored points and who won. That's what we love about sports. The real world is messy and ambiguous. Brad needed an orderly universe. He could not yet go beyond what his whole society took as a given: Jesus was the son of God, and the father imparted to him the ultimate purpose and results of life and death and beyond. He started to read the Bible more intensely. Soon he confirmed his earlier conclusion that the Old Testament merely told an interesting history of Jesus' people. Even if God did drop in here or there and gave Moses some platitudes, profound truths were not revealed. He now felt sure that the Torah should not be included in the Holy Christian Bible.

Jesus, on the other hand, gave a very clear, consistent and startling world view: This earth, this life, this split second of cosmic time—this discouraging reality is not the important reality. True being is not physical but spiritual, coming after death, in God's vast ethereal kingdom, life everlasting. This life is an outer hallway, a training ground, a fetal development. We must learn to love thine enemy, let him smite the other cheek, shun treasures where moths and rust doth corrupt, even your life—"for he who saves his life shall lose it. But he who loses his life for my sake shall save it." And Jesus didn't just talk the talk, he walked the walk. No temple building—he preached on a hillside. No deluxe camel or fine clothes. The best lodging we hear about is that crib in the stable. And when Peter, trying to guard Jesus, hacked off a Roman ear, Jesus said, "He who lives by the sword shall perish by the sword."

Troubling. Very troubling. How could a young man, full of the joys of flesh and peanut butter and motorcycles be equally thrilled by this world-renouncing religion? Simple—each of us is quite comfortable with his own contradictions. Brad felt his simple pleasures were venial sins and did not tie his soul to this earth the way hatred or hurting people would. What is inexcusable hypocrisy in someone else becomes acceptable compromise in ourselves. Which does not mean we're wrong about the other guy. Brad saw more and more clearly how unchristian his Christian world was. Here were all these millionaire church deacons, who must have known that Jesus said, "It is easier for a camel to go though the eye of a needle than for a rich man to enter Heaven." Yet they were sure St. Peter would usher them in. The minister of his church, who last year was given a raise, a new car and a new house, was leaving because another church offered him a higher salary.

So Brad was changing from a premature kid into a mature youth, still jitterbugging and cheering at football games, still caressing Kay (who teased him about his high school dates), yet seeing his world with a more piercing eye, and wondering what Jesus would say about these Christian folk.

Although Kay wanted to limit herself to teasing about girlfriends, feeling it wrong to stifle his social development, sometimes jealousy would sneak in—"Do you kiss Nancy the way you kiss me?"

"No, really, just a peck good night. I feel guilty enough about adultery with you. I don't need some little girl on my conscience. You know, I try not to mention your sleeping with your husband, but it hurts."

"That's all we're doing — sleeping. He's too tired from screwing his secretary to grab me." Brad assumed that Kay, like everyone else, knew about the secretary, but he was startled to hear her say it so casually.

"Does it bother you?"

"Not anymore. Even before you, I stopped caring. Since you, it gives me a good excuse for us."

Chapter IV

*K*AY was raised in a very affluent, but not filthy rich, family. She went through expensive private schools, coming out the other end a casually educated young woman. During school, she wasn't part of the "in" group or the "out" group. Those two are really very small. The large middle group doesn't actually pay much attention to them. They hang out and party and are quite content with themselves. Kay had been successful there, with her easy acceptance of and enjoyment of people as they are. She liked her classes without any thought toward dedicated, scholarly pursuits. She emerged ready for the next phase of life—wife and mother.

She met a tall, handsome, suave, ambitious southerner, who was happy to marry into a well-off, influential family. After a couple of years of happy marriage, her husband's job and secretary kept him away a lot, and she settled into running a big house, raising a child, and reading in bed, until she found something better in bed than books.

Brad, meanwhile, had reached the spring of his senior year in high school. His strong insistence that Jesus meant what he said, and that Christians must follow what he said, would not have upset his place in the world, except for history. In fact, his father bragged about his religious son the way he intended to brag about him as an athlete. But history's heavy boots stomped in. It was the spring of 1942. Pearl Harbor had been attacked. We were at war. Brad would soon turn eighteen and be compelled to register for the draft. He struggled with the problem of pacifism—could a faithful follower of Jesus pick up a gun and consciously and conscientiously kill an enemy? The country, of course, didn't care what Jesus would do. A good Christian would automatically be patriotic, and a shirker was a traitor. To be more accurate, the country knew that God approved of fighting this evil enemy. Given the horrifying nature of this enemy, that conclusion followed easily. But not easy for Brad.

Especially as this was a "good" war. After all, Japan, the rapist of China, pulled a sneak attack on Pearl Harbor. Brad was not yet aware that in the barbaric game of conquest, America had grabbed dozens of islands all across the Pacific Ocean, including the huge Philippines, five thousand miles away from California on Japan's doorstep. Japan wanted that Pacific Empire. The U.S.A. knew it would have to fight to hold it. In his diary, Stimson, secretary of war at that time (yes, we had a War Department until politicians decided a Defense Department sounded better, as it could not be accused of aggression), Stimson wrote that two weeks before Pearl Harbor, a cabinet meeting discussed how to goad Japan into attacking, as our isolationist country was antiwar. They decided to send Japan an ultimatum to get out of China or face an oil embargo. None of this was common knowledge, nor publicized. After Pearl Harbor, it would not have mattered. The ruthless Japanese (and they were) had stabbed us in the back. A conflict raged within Brad between Jesus and patriotism.

The new minister, young, intelligent, well educated, listened carefully and thoughtfully to everyone. After the Thursday evening choir rehearsal, Brad passed him in the hall. "Reverend, was Jesus a flat-out pacifist?" The young minister was thinking. Before he answered, Brad continued, "If so, should a true Christian refuse to kill? Should he 'love thine enemy,' even when thine enemy is trying to kill you?"

The minister thought some more, then said, "That's a tough one. I know how I feel, but I want it to come out of my mouth the right way. I'll get back to you. Soon." Brad watched him slowly walk down the hall. Then the minister turned around and yelled to Brad, "I'll get back to you on Sunday!"

The preliminary organ music, prayers and hymns concluded, and the minister ascended the pulpit. "A few days ago, a member of our congregation asked me if Jesus was a flat-out pacifist, and if so, would a true Christian refuse to kill under any circumstances. Today, this is no academic, theological question. Some of our congregation already have their uniforms and guns. Soon millions of Americans will be shooting at and dropping bombs on millions of soldiers and civilians. Were I to tell you that this is sinful in the eyes of God and implore you to refuse to be part of this carnage and to walk into Hitler's and Hiroshima's bullets with love for thine enemies—well, I'm sure there would be a new minister up here next Sunday. But please believe me, if I thought that was the whole truth, I would say so, and you could go ahead and fire me.

"Let's first look at the complicated relationship between the Old and New Testaments. We tend to think of them as two seamless parts of one book, the one and only holy book, the Bible. The Old Testament tells us of God's special relationship with the Jews. God gives them miracles to free them from Egypt. The Jews are his chosen people. God gives them commandments, telling them how to behave and how to worship him. They are a warlike people and God helps them in battle. Their leaders are not always noble soldiers. David sets up Bathsheba's husband to get killed in battle so he can have her. Jacob, the man who became Israel, tricked his father into giving him his brother's birthright. But God sticks with his chosen people and promises to send a messiah to be king of kings.

"The New Testament seems to be a seamless continuation, with Mary, a Jewish woman, giving virgin birth to the messiah. But the story takes a strange turn. As Jesus grows up, he sees the religious leaders as corrupt as some of the Old Testament characters, in cahoots with the Romans, milking their own people in the synagogue at the money changing tables. He chastises them. He shuns the synagogue, preaching in an open field. He is no David, no Joshua, no Solomon or Saul. He certainly will not be king of kings. 'My kingdom is not of this earth,' he proclaims. The message is love, even love thine enemies, turn the other cheek to be hit again. The Jews, of course, reject him. His improbable pilgrimage into our gentile world over the last two thousand years is a very different story, to be told another time. Was Jesus a pacifist? Certainly. The ruthless rulers from Rome conquered his country, but there isn't the slightest hint of his calling for armed resistance. It's always fight hate with love, fight evil with love, fight force with love.

"Today, several small church groups preach pacifism and their members will not go to war. Our government respects their beliefs and, as fellow Christians, we certainly should too. What about you and me? I, for one, although I'm aware of our foreign policy blunders which helped create this horror, cannot turn the world over to the Nazis. So I will kill, if called upon to do so. At the same time, I'm deeply troubled that I might be failing Jesus. Let us pray. Dear Jesus, help us see that we are justified in fighting this war only if victory means bringing your love into the world, only if we help our enemies feel the beauty of that love. Amen." Brad got his answer.

That evening, having finished his homework, he went into the living room, where his father was listening to and cursing at a liberal radio reporter. "Did you hear that crap?" the father asked. "Why doesn't the goddam commie move to Russia?"

"Dad,"said Brad, "there's something I must tell you. I'm going to register as a conscientious objector."

"What the fuck is that?"

"It means I can't join the war."

"For Christsake, are you a coward?"

"It is for Christ's sake, and you know I'm not a coward."

His father shouted, "If you won't fight, it's the same thing as being a coward! You know I don't like killing Germans, especially for kikes and commies. But the Japs attacked us and we've got to kill them. Don't do this to me! What am I going to tell the guys at the office? Do *you* know how this will make me look? After all I've done for you, this is the thanks I get? Don't do this to me!"

Brad knew his father would show no sympathy. He never did when something really mattered to Brad. The son remembered how he had to plead for an allowance, twenty-five cents per week.

"Why?" his father would ask. "Don't I give you more than that?"

"Yes, Dad, and I'm grateful. But I want to learn how to handle my own money." Then, every Friday, instead of giving Brad his allowance, he'd reach into his pocket and bring out a closed fist of change, and ask, "Will you settle for what's in my hand?"

"No, please, just give me my quarter."

"Are you sure? There's probably more here."

"No thanks, Dad, just my quarter."

The fist would open and the father would say, "Well, look at that! Forty-seven cents. You really lost out." Brad could never make him understand that he had not lost out.

As the full impact of Brad's statement hit the father, he flew into a rage. "What am I going to tell my friends—my son's a Jesus freak who wants to kiss Hitler's ass instead of shoot him? You know what they'll do with you? They'll throw you in jail, that's what they'll do! And I'll have to tell everyone you'd rather rot in jail than defend your country. I didn't raise my son to be a traitor!"

"I'm sorry, Dad, but I have no choice. I must do this." Brad felt a mountain of guilt a week later when his father suddenly died of a heart attack. The son thought he was the main cause, not just the last straw, because he did not know about all the other straws. Despite doctors' warnings, the father ate nothing but artery-clogging specialties. He never met a cholesterol he didn't like. One of the reasons he had Brad say he wasn't home was the fear of bill collectors. He owed car payments, rent, gas and electricity, telephone, department stores, the local grocer, and borrowed money. He not only padded his expense account in the accepted manner, but way beyond the legal limit, and lived in constant fear of the audit department. He had had a minor heart attack five years earlier and not changed his bad eating habits one bite. Lastly, a month ago, the police found him parked in his car with an eleven-year-old black boy, and he was paying (owing) a lawyer to avoid a trial. All debts were paid by death. Brad's older brother cleaned up the mess. Kay insisted he stay in one of her many rooms. He finished high school and looked for a temporary job until the Draft Board called, as he would soon turn nineteen.

He wanted physical work and got a job at a factory which manufactured huge sewer pipes. Being part of the adult working world gave him confidence that he could deal with whatever would soon be thrust upon him. The first day, the stupid foreman put him to work rolling a piece of steel. Some piece! It was twelve feet long, eight feet wide, and a half inch thick! There were three "rollers," sixteen feet long and two feet in diameter. Two rollers were stationary and the third could be lowered between them. By pulleys and clamps, you inserted this huge sheet of steel between them and rotated the rollers, slightly curving the steel. Then you lowered the third roller a little and ran it through again, curving it some more, and so forth until it was a round pipe. Well, they got Brad started, but no one told him how gently to lower the third roller. The first few times he ran the steel through didn't curve it very much, so he lowered the third roller several notches. Before he realized what was happening, he had wrapped the steel around the roller and the "off" switch jammed. "Help!" he yelled. It took them three days to untangle the steel.

But on the whole, the factory adopted the youngster, and he earned his twenty-four cents per hour. One vivid memory of those months stayed with him forever. Earl, a silent, expressionless man, operated a "press." This imposing machine had a "table," a solid hunk of hardened steel three feet high and two feet in diameter. Four feet above it was a duplicate. The two pieces were so perfectly engineered that, when together, you could not insert a piece of paper between them. Earl was highly skilled at compressing and bending anything into any shape required. Slowly, he'd lower and raise the upper weight like a sculptor. Then every night, when the five o'clock whistle blew, Earl would raise it the full four feet, put his watch on the table, and let the weight free fall! He'd stop it an inch from his watch. The whole factory would shudder. Still expressionless, Earl would raise the weight a foot, take his watch and go home. One night, when he had just picked up his watch, a simple-minded worker said, "Earl, will you do that with my watch?" A slight hint of contempt crossed Earl's face as he held out his hand. He placed the man's watch on the table. The massive cylinder of steel came crashing down like a bomb from a plane and sounded like an explosion as it pounded the table and shook the floor. Without looking at the man, Earl raised it two feet and went home. The man stood there staring in disbelief. He probably would have shouted curses and threats if he saw mangled metal and glass, but there was nothing. Nothing! Not even a little dust! He stared some more, then went home.

Chapter V

*K*AY and Dex felt a deep sense of duty to help their country. She volunteered for the Red Cross. He volunteered for the Army. But they both loved Brad and comforted him in his time of trouble. The trouble finally arrived, a letter to report to the Draft Board. Five middle-aged and elderly men sat behind a table. Brad stood in front of them. The one in the middle held a letter Brad had written to the board.

"It says here you want to register as a conscientious objector on Christian grounds. Are you a member of one of those weird sects, like Quakers or seven day adventures?"

"No, sir. I'm not really tied to any particular denomination. I just feel strongly that Jesus doesn't want me to purposely go out and kill people."

"Now tell me, young feller," the man said with the voice of his father, "how the hell do you think we're gonna win this war if we excuse every yella belly who comes in here and says he doesn't wanna fight? We've got jails for guys like you! Out of 68,000 people in our great city, you're the only one who came in here with this crap. Are you going to ruin our record?"

"Sir, I love my country and am very grateful for all my

country has given me. I know the Nazi government and the Japanese government are horrible. I know the world will be a better place if we win, and I pray that we do. But Jesus will not let me be a part of the killing."

The man, face red with rage, leaned forward, hands on the table, elbows jutting out to the side, and yelled, "If you're afraid of getting hurt in the war, wait till you see what they do to you in prison! Even crooks hate cowards and traitors. And they love young boys! You're afraid of getting your ass shot off? Wait till you get your ass torn open in jail!"

"Howard, Howard!" said a man at the end of the table. "That is completely out of bounds! The law specifically deals with conscientious objectors, and this board must and will follow the rules!" He turned to Brad. "Now, young man, let me give you an alternative. Instead of wasting away in jail and costing the taxpayers money for no good purpose, you could be saving lives, healing people who are victims of war. We can put you in the Army Medical Corps. You can dodge bullets in the front lines while you bandage wounds, thus showing love and proving to Howard you're no coward."

Brad was very surprised and asked, "Can I do that?"

"Yes. Will you?"

So Brad became a soldier with a caduceus on his lapel. First there was the induction in a room at City Hall. He and a small group of men stood naked for a physical. A doctor came down the row quickly examining eyes, ears, throat, heart and genitals. Then he said, "Turn around, bend over and spread your cheeks." While the doctor examined Brad's anus, he asked, "Have you had any operations?"

"Just my tonsils out."

"Yes," said the doctor, "I can see that." Brad really needed that little chance to smile.

If the sewer pipe factory had opened Brad's eyes to the blue-collar man, the Army would expose him to the whole range of the American male, from nineteen to over fifty years old; from the Mississippi swamps to the Minnesota snows; from prestigious universities to no high school; from every profession, religion, lifestyle, size and shape, personality and ancestry—except African. America, before WWII, while quite tolerant of immigrants from anywhere, was profoundly prejudiced against those Americans whose ancestry went back many generations—blacks. Not only in the south, where a black man could be lynched for just looking at a white woman, but throughout the nation. So the armed forces completely segregated blacks and whites. Aside from that, this drafted civilian Army was more broad-based and inclusive than any before or since. They far outnumbered the regular soldiers from before the war. Some highly educated men were not officers and some hardly educated men were. Six weeks of basic training was supposed to turn them into athletes who could climb walls, crawl under barbed wire, run up hills and down stairs. Under the one-hundred-degree Arkansas sun, with a full sixty-pound field backpack, they marched twenty-five miles. A long line of ambulances followed them, picking up the guys who dropped. For Brad, it was no different than football practice. For many, like the forty-year-old saxophone player who had spent his life sitting on a chair and moving only his fingers, it was unbearable. Most of his 240 pounds rested around his waist. When dismissed, he would sit on his bunk for a long time, staring at nothing, softly repeating, "I can't do this. I can't do this one more day." Being the Medical Corps, they did not train with guns, but did endure battlefield barrages. While crawling under live machine gun fire, a wild kid behind Brad grabbed his foot and yelled, "Slow down and enjoy it! These might be the only bullets that will miss you!" It seemed like forever before Brad freed his foot.

A burly sergeant gave them lessons in the martial arts. After each complicated maneuver, which they did not understand, he would say, "If you forget this, kick him in the balls." They all got the message about the best martial arts technique. The sergeant called this puny, scared recruit out of line and said, "Sock me on the jaw."

The kid, standing trembling at stiff attention, said, "No sir, sergeant sir, no sir. I can't do that, sir!"

With a surly grin, the sergeant pointed to his chin. "Come on, lay one on me. Right here." The sergeant expected the usual round house, which he would grab and almost break the kid's arm as he threw him over his shoulder. But the kid, still ramrod at attention, trembling and pleading, suddenly shot his fist straight up, and the sergeant was out cold.

With basic training almost completed, the entire company, all four platoons, were assembled on the parade grounds. They stood at parade rest. The four corporals snapped salutes at the lieutenant and shouted, "First-platoon-all-present-or-accounted-for, second-platoon-all-present-or-accounted-for," etc. Then the lieutenant, under the bored eyes of the major and his staff and friends, paraded the company around the field. Much to everyone's amazement, the major asked, "Does any recruit want to parade the company?" It turns out that he made this offer because he hated the lieutenant and hoped some recruit would fuck up, thus amusing the spectators and embarrassing the lieutenant. Equally amazing, the timid young man who had decked the sergeant yelled, "I would like to, sir!"

"Front and center, Private," said the major. "The company's yours."

The young man barked, "Company, attention! Right face! Forward march! First platoon to the rear march, second platoon to the rear march, third platoon to the rear march, fourth platoon to the rear march." Then he reversed the order, bringing them together again. He continued to fan them out, circle them, intertwine them, and finally left them exactly as he had found them.

"Where the hell did you learn that?" demanded the major.

"From our fine lieutenant, sir!" smiled the recruit.

"Cut the crap, soldier! Answer me."

"Well, also sir, I was the marching band director in college."

After basic training, almost all of these men would be sent to infantry units to be trained as "company aid men." They would accompany the troops into battle to care for the wounded. A small number would be sent for medical and surgical training to work in hospitals. At a bivouac talk session, the recruits were asked what they preferred to do, a gesture to make them feel listened to. Out of 200 soldiers, only Brad and four others wanted to be company aid men. More than the adventure of being in battle, he wanted to prove to himself that cowardice played no part in being a conscientious objector. So he was surprised and dismayed when he saw his name posted on a small list of men who would be moving out in two days. Obviously, these were going to technical school to train for hospital work. They were heartily congratulated by the others. Brad asked to see the "bird" colonel who ran the camp.

This colonel personified the "old soldier," fat and fifty, puffing on a cigar. Behind his back, they called him colon-el, labeling him an asshole. In the outer office, Brad could hear him shouting at his aide, "What the fuck does he want to see me about, and why the fuck would I want to see him?" Brad had evidently impressed the aide, who convinced the colonel. "All right," he shouted, "send the little shit in!"

Brad saluted and said, "I'm sorry to bother you, sir, but rumor has it that—"

"Rumor?" roared the colonel. "Whois spreading rumors? I'll have your head!"

"Sorry, sir, I said it badly. It's just obvious that the small group shipping out is going to hospital training school, and my name is on it."

43

"So?"

"So I was one of the very few who wanted to be a company aid man, and I'm hoping you would take me off that list."

The colonel yelled to his aid, "Get me this kid's record." He went through the papers, including Brad's high marks on the Army intelligence test, and said, "Let me tell you something, kid. There's nothing I'd like better than to see you college-type brats get your ass shot off, and that goes double for conscientious objectors. But we've got a war to win. So we stick the dumb ones up front to get shot and send you smart-asses to school. And that's where you're going. Now get the hell out of here!" Brad's present furious rage would, decades later, be replaced by thanks for saving his life.

Brad wrote all this in one of his frequent letters to Kay. He always ended his letters with a love poem to her. This time, he also included this poem:

> Some of the power
> to bend black backs over cotton,
> to hack the heathen out of the Holy Land,
> to cheat at reading tea leaves with China,
> came from the Prince of Peace
> The crosspiece of the handle
> makes the sword a crucifix. Church and
> churchmen never quite managed to pull Christ off.
> He hid on some dull spot on the blade and
> forced their lips,
> in crazy contradiction to crashing fists, to form
> "Love even enemies."
> Son of God, or no, who cares? his least love
> caressed more than our most.
> When we, the white world, have our handcuffs
> stolen, sit inside jail looking inward, with proper
> pride in free minds which fertilized soil and seeded
> clouds,

we will not know(and neither will the jailer) the
greatest gift we left was the song we sang, the song of
love.

As always, Kay answered him immediately, congratulating
him on truly becoming a real poet. She wrote to him every
week. Only someone who has been in the Army can know
how much those letters are valued.

While the 173rd General Hospital was being assembled to
go to England, the Army was trying to transform Brad and
others into nurses in two months. Classes were two hours
long, two in the morning and two in the afternoon. A sergeant
stood in the back of the classroom, ready to poke anyone who
seemed not to be paying attention, and give a strong whack
to anyone falling asleep. The students memorized all the
organs and bones in the body, learned the uses of many drugs,
put bandages and splints on each other, drew each other's
blood, and practiced artificial respiration. The better
students, including Brad, were taught to "scrub" and put on
sterile caps, gowns and gloves, and quickly identify all
surgical instruments, so they could work in the operating
room. Four of them became fast friends and referred to
themselves as the "4Bs" — Brad, Bill, Ben and Buck.

Bill and Buck had been pre-med students. Ben had been a
graduate student in sociology. He was an atheist
conscientious objector, disgusted with the barbarism of these
"advanced" nations destroying each other over real estate. He
was bitter, and grateful that the other three Bs laughed and
smiled for him.

Medical training school provided wonderful opportunities
for needling — "Hey, Brad, I really have trouble drawing
blood. Lend me your arm." "I'd love to, but Bill has smaller
veins for better practice." Or "Come on, guys, it's chow time!
Take these splints off my arms and legs!"

As four budding intellectuals, they got into serious

discussions, such as Bill challenging Ben's eating vegetables with a spoon. "Let me set you straight on history," Ben responded. "As the human race extended our tool-making genius into food consumption, we invented a stabber, the fork, a cutter, the knife, and a scooper, the spoon. You stabbed meat, you cut big things, and you scooped up little things. Then some lazy bastard, instead of putting down the steak stabber and picking up the pea scooper, used his fork to scoop up the peas. It wasn't easy, but that never stops a lazy guy. He was powerful, so nobody laughed. In fact, they meekly imitated him, and it became the fashionable way. I say, let's get back to the correct method."

Buck took up the theme—"You remind me of Ben Franklin, who, after his kite and lightning success, was invited by the French Academy of Science to write a paper on some esoteric subject. He replied, 'Why don't you guys research something worthwhile, like how to make farts smell sweeter?'"

"Oh, come on," said Bill. "He never did that!"

"Scout's honor," insisted Buck. "Look it up."

Bill thought for a moment, then asked, "Do you weigh less before or after you fart? I mean, you get rid of something, so you should weigh less. But you let the helium out of a balloon and it weighs more." There followed a heated discussion of weight and mass and volume displacement and the atomic weight of farts.

The intense training finally ended. They sat up all night in railroad cars, were reminded that "loose lips sink ships," and were loaded straight from the Boston Railroad station onto what once was a luxury ocean liner, called the *Queen Mary*. Thousands of soldiers crammed into every possible space. Canvas bunks were stacked four high, so close that rolling over meant bumping the guy above you. During the train trip and the two days waiting on board the ship, Bill kept complaining, "I know I'm going to be seasick." The magnificent ship was fast enough to outrun submarines, so it had already crossed the Atlantic many times unescorted, as it would this time. Buck woke up about 5:00 AM, glanced out the porthole and noticed the Boston harbor docks receding. "We're moving!" he yelled. Bill was immediately seasick.

Life on board ship was a slow walk all the way around all the decks, starting on the top deck and spiraling down to the bottom. This three-hour walk occurred twice a day, from 7:00 AM to 10:00 AM and from 2:00 PM to 5:00 PM. At the end of your morning stroll, you held out your mess kit and got oatmeal on one side and ham, scrambled eggs and bread on the other. The coffee tasted of aluminum from your aluminum mug. At the end of your afternoon promenade, you got a big scoop of ice cream. If you were lucky, it landed on the vegetables instead of on the meat and potatoes.

Cleanliness was not a wartime priority on board ship. Everything smelled as dirty as it was. Many battalions had used the "life preservers" as pillows, seats, back rests and to stand on to spot a friend. All flotation quality had been squashed out of them. You carried this disgusting object for the above reasons and to avoid a chewing out by an officer. That is, except for Bill. He always wore his in the correct manner. "Go ahead and laugh," he'd say, "but when the ship goes down, don't grab hold of me!"

One day Buck, tired of hearing this, grabbed a spare life preserver and said, "Hey, Bill! Watch this." He threw it overboard. It didn't even pause at the surface. Bill's security sank with the sinking savior, as he stared at the empty ocean where the life preserver went down. He still wore his, but avoided the subject. The only further mention of flotation devices was when a strange-looking soldier from a different outfit walked up to the 4Bs and asked, "If you fell overboard, wouldn't you want someone to throw you a life preserver?" They nodded to dismiss him. He said, "Then let us pray." When they turned away, he walked away.

Brad said, "I'll pray for all of us without anyone overboard."

The 173rd General Hospital ended up in the lovely, rolling countryside near Chester, England. On the whole, the "Yanks" were welcomed, although somewhat resented, as an American private earned the equivalent of a British major, and all GI's came on strong with women, thus the popular complaint that the Yanks were "overpaid, oversexed and over here."

Long lines of one-story concrete buildings housed the hospital. The troops lived sixteen to a Quonset hut, eight double bunks. A Quonset hut was metal half sphere with a concrete floor. For a mattress, each soldier received a burlap sack and was escorted to a pile of straw. In the middle of the hut stood a cylindrical cast-iron stove. They were instructed how to build a fire: twigs on top of paper and a small amount of coal. When the coal caught fire, add more coal. But they figured out a better way: fill the stove with coal. Pour almost all of a big bottle of lighter fluid into the top. Use what's left as a fuse across the floor and out the door. Match—boom! The stove would leap off the floor and every piece of coal was burning. Everyone rushed back in and jumped in bed before a puzzled officer came by to trace the noise.

The hospital's obvious purpose was to handle the wounded from the invasion of the continent, still a year away. So the last half of 1943 and the first half of 1944 was a leisurely time. The bugler had played trumpet for a famous jazz band, so, as the soldiers didn't have to fall in for roll call when it rained, he played a wah-wah rendition of "Stormy Weather," and they dozed off for a few more minutes. If you wanted to taste the war, you had to get a pass to London, where bombs were blasting away. The Nazi air force, the Luftwaffe, had been driven from the sky. But the Germans invented the V1 , a small, fast, pilotless jet airplane, actually a bomb with wings, designed to run out of fuel over London. When you heard the motor stop, it was time to get scared. Then the Germans perfected the V2, a genuine rocket which ascended miles and came down too fast to be heard or shot at. After the war, the Russians and Americans punished the politicians and generals, but raced each other to catch and welcome the rocket scientists.

It felt strange to be touring London Bridge and Buckingham Palace while an occasional buzz bomb fell from the sky. Brad was sitting in a movie theater when suddenly the whole building shook from a nearby explosion. An Englishman next to him said with a calm smile, "Close one, eh?" Iron, stacked bunk beds lined the walls of subway stations. People slept soundly as trains roared past. Nighttime meant complete blackout, and many doorways provided a little seclusion for a GI and a girl to make out standing up.

The best part of Brad's pass was the train ride back to camp with a delightful, distinguished Englishman who personified British charm with the following story: "This Englishman was riding along on a train with a Yank, just like us. The Yank tried telling jokes, but the Brit just didn't get them. So the Yank's jokes degenerated down to this: 'Mary had a little dress that split right up the side, and every time she took a step, you'd see her little hide.' When the Englishman got home to his dinner, he said to his family, 'Oh, I rode with this funny American chap today, and he told me this: Mary had a little dress that split right up the front, and every time she took a step...oh, I say, no, that can't be right.'"

The hospital waited, underused. Only ordinary illnesses and accidents needed medical attention. You could enjoy canned orange juice with medicinal alcohol—200 proof. You could do crazy things like filling a 100 cc syringe with ether and, with a cigarette lighter in front of it, shoot a flame ten feet across the bow of an unsuspecting friend. You could inhale laughing gas and not feel funny, although you laughed until your face and sides hurt.

And there was time for an unexpected operation. We mentioned that Brad had an unusually long foreskin. Often the end became irritated. The doctor said he really should be circumcised. This caused much laughter and many jokes. Brad said, "OK, but only Ben and Buck work the operation— no female nurses." Brad brought a mirror so he could watch. The novocaine hurt like hell, but after that they had fun. The inside of the penis is spongy material which fills with blood for an erection When the doctor had cut off the skin all the way around the base of the head, the remaining skin no longer restricted the stretchy inside, so the doctor said, "Shall I leave it like this?" and stretched it out to more than a foot. They all shrieked, "Yeah! Yeah!." However, he had to tuck it all back in and sew the skin to the head.

"In the night," the doctor said, "when you get an erection, call for the nurse and she'll give you a shot."

"An erection!" yelled Brad incredulously "That's the last thing on my mind."

"It will happen," insisted the doctor, "and it will hurt like a son of a bitch." And it sure did, with Brad screaming, "Go down, you stupid prick!" In addition to the pain of healing, the head experienced the strange, new, uncomfortable world of clothing. Brad walked around with his hands in the pockets of his robe, holding his pajama pants out in front, enduring endless giggles and kidding.

Of course, he wrote all about this to Kay, who teasingly responded, "Do you feel a little bit Jewish now? Feel a little closer to the Old Testament? Closer to Jesus, who must have been circumcised? Is your friend apprehensive about sticking his head out into this war-torn world? I can't wait to play with my new toy!"

Bill had desperately wanted to work in the operating room with Brad, Ben and Buck, but he was assigned to a surgical ward. One night Brad was covering the OR while Ben and Buck went into town. They came back early and popped in on

Brad. Ben came up with an idea. (People, especially young people, often fail to see the line between kidding and cruelty.) "Bill always wanted to work in the OR. Why don't I lie on the table, covered, as an emergency operation. Buck will hide. Call Bill's head nurse to let him come scrub while you circulate." A u-frame often covered a patient's face on the operating table.

Imagine Bill's thrill and excitement as he arrived and began scrubbing, a long process, starting with fingernails and ending at the elbows, then carefully dressing in cap, mask, gown and gloves. He tried to ignore Ben's moans and groans. Bill asked, "What's wrong with him?"

"They don't know," Brad answered."They'll just cut him open and see what they find." He gave Bill difficult instructions, including threading thick sutures through thin needle eyes. Brad whispered to Ben, "I'm running out." Ben groaned louder and began to move. "Whoa, steady boy," Brad said, trying to hold Ben's legs.

Bill panicked with outrage. "Where are the goddam doctors!?" Ben became really violent.

"Sorry, Bill," Brad said, "you're going to have to break your scrub and help me hold him." That crushed Bill. He knew it meant starting all over again. So Bill grabbed Ben's legs, Brad held his chest, keeping his face covered, and Bill worked against both of them. They struggled and struggled and over they all went onto the floor.

Bill trembled and shouted, "Oh my God! Oh my God! What if the doctors come in now? They'll court martial us!" They got Ben back on the table. Then more violent struggle and again two nurses were rolling around on the floor with the patient!

Buck came out of hiding and asked, "What the hell are you guys doing?"

Ben emerged and, answered, "We're just wrestling." Bill stood stunned for almost a minute before he could accept the event. Slowly he pulled each glove off as if peeling the skin from his hands. He slammed each piece of clothing against the wall. They were still laughing as he left, then quickly realized the cruelty. They spent the next two weeks trying everything possible to make amends, but Bill would not even look at them.

During this time, Kay provided desperately needed support for Brad. He missed her so much. She wrote to him every week without fail. She sent very long, newsy letters about his hometown— sometimes sad news about a high school buddy, sometimes glad news about the varsity beating an arch-rival. Dex was a bombardier. He was shot down on his first mission before he even dropped one bomb, but he made it back to friendly territory. Brad felt sorry that Kay's food was rationed while he watched some soldiers throw away half-eaten meat. She wrote long, detailed descriptions and critiques of the books she read, giving him at least some second-hand background of the literary scene. He had become ravenous for knowledge and shared with her his voracious reading in science, math, philosophy and history, which didn't much interest her, but benefitted him by putting his thoughts down on paper. He wrote, "Did you know that Einstein's relativity says you could take a certain space journey and come back in two years by your calendar. But everything on earth would have gone through fifty years! You'd be younger than your daughter!" And he always included a poem he had written for her:

> Summer starts the same as "singing,"
> same as "stars, sky, sea and sun."
> Summer starts the same as flinging
> waves of me at you for fun.
>
> Summer ends just like "September,"
> "cooler, darker, older, bier."

Summer ends like falling timber,
losing hold when you're not near.

She asked him about any contact with the people of
England. She was, of course, fishing for any female
acquaintances. He replied that the British complained that the
Americans were "overpaid, oversexed and over here." He told
her about the delightful man on the train. He knew what she
wanted to know, so he told her about Betty. This woman,
twenty-five years old, worked in the hospital linen room. She
had not seen her husband, a soldier in North Africa, for two
years. A quiet girl of average looks, she went out of her way
to talk with Brad. When she learned that he was going into
town that night to see a movie, she said, "Oh, I want to see that
film too. I'll see you there." At the theater, she got in line
behind him and they sat together. After the show, she asked
him to walk her home. She led him into an orchard, sat down
on the grass and said, "I can't take you home. I live with my
mother-in-law." She pulled him down beside her. He hadn't
realized how much he missed holding a woman until he
kissed her and felt her breast. When he reached for the
bottom of her skirt, she stopped his hand and said, "We can't
do it tonight—I've got the curse. We'll do it next week." She
took out his penis and rubbed it between her breasts until he
came.

For the next few days, he felt ashamed and guilty. *Here I
am*, he thought, *supposedly a good Christian, and again about
to screw another man's wife while the poor bastard is fighting in
North Africa.* So he conquered his lust and wrote her a warm,
grateful regret, making sure not to imply that she should feel
guilty. He did not want to cast the first stone. That letter
greatly pleased Kay.

Brad also wrote Kay about an incident involving his friend
Buck. Buck was very angry when he learned that a soldier had

died because an ambulance was not available. The ambulance was carrying a captain's dog to the vet. Buck wrote to Rex Westbrook, a famous newspaper and radio reporter. A while later, Buck got a phone call from Westbrook: "I'm going to use your story on my radio program this Sunday night. Don't worry. I'll make sure the Army brass don't beat on you. For every colonel they've got, I've got a general, and if they've got two-star generals, I've got three-star generals. So just sit tight." The story caused a national uproar, and nothing happened to Buck.

Finally, his letter told Kay that, although Jesus' earth-rejecting religion provided tremendous intellectual comfort and a deep feeling of connecting him to the real Universe with an everlasting role in it, he ached for a woman. So when a buxom nurse invited him into the storage room, not to take inventory, he went. As Army regulations forbade enlisted men to fraternize with officers, and nurses were officers, they did not get together often.

Brad had no idea how vulnerable his religion was. His agile mind demanded cosmological consistency, although he would not have known such fancy words. Jesus was the only exposure he had to meet the requirement. But as he read science, history, and philosophy, he slowly and painfully began to doubt that his beautiful Jesus knew God, or there was a God to know. Ben continually tried to push him out the church door. He would say, "Brad, do you know how Cain and Abel got wives? You see, the author had a dilemma: to continue the human race, Eve's sons either had to fuck mom, or mom had to produce daughters for fucking—incest either way. So the author says, with a straight face, they went to a nearby town and took wives!"

"Well," Brad would say defensively, "the Old Testament is not Jesus."

"Hey," Ben would push, "the OT is ninety percent of your Holy Bible, and Jesus said not one jot or one tittle, etc. Do you know what God told Abraham to do? If you really worship me, cut your son's throat! What kind of a sadistic bastard would say that? And we praise Abe because he was willing to do it! Some father. Some religion. I taught public school for one year. The state law required a Christian service in home room. We had to read a small section of the Old Testament without comment, then the class would recite Jesus' prayer. Most teachers always read the twenty-first Psalm. I read all the juicy parts, like Lot's daughters getting him drunk to fuck him so he could have sons. The principal pleaded with me not to, but I feigned indignation and demanded to know if he was calling the Holy Bible salacious! You can bet no student was ever late for my home room."

"OK," Brad admitted, "the Old Testament is a hodgepodge of Jewish history, early naive attempts to explain the universe, and a search for a moral compass. But Jesus is simple and consistent: You must learn to love everyone for they are all God's children, and nothing in this world, where moth and rust doth corrupt, is worth fighting for. You prepare your soul for its non-physical life after death, as Jesus' kingdom is not of this earth."

Ben shook his head. "Yes, consistent, but unfortunately absurd. This soul stuff is just silly wishful thinking. We are so outraged that this magnificent, self-conscious, knowledgeable person lasts only a quick tick of eternal time, that we make believe this rotting carcass isn't really me—I'm really something else, a non-physical, eternal being. It's so pathetic."

"But Ben," pleaded Brad, "I feel it so strong, just as strong as I feel the sun on my skin."

"Brad, you can SEE the sunlight, you can see the SUN! This God and his Jesus have been hiding for two thousand years. Why?"

Brad insisted, "I see them everywhere—in trees and flowers and birds."

"No you don't—you see trees and flowers and birds. Where are God and Jesus while millions of kids are starving and Hitler is killing his chosen people? Are they too busy helping some basketball player who crossed himself make a foul shot?"

"We're just not able to understand the ways of God."

"And He's not able to teach us?"

"Ben, Jesus is my strength. Life would lose its meaning without him. All the joy I get from you guys, and it's a lot, is nothing compared to the joy I get from Jesus."

Ben smiled and said, "I know we gotta go, but let me tell you one more story. Bertold Brecht wrote a play about Galileo. The grand inquisitor is threatening him. Galileo insists he's a good son of the church, but he can't doubt what he sees in his telescope. He begs the bishop to take a look. The grand inquisitor replies, 'Were I to look into your telescope and see what you see, it would only mean that the Devil had captured my eyes the way he has captured yours.' It's a perfectly valid position—and Brad, it's totally idiotic. I'm convinced that religious convictions generate the worst sins in this world. We can muddle through if we accept our ignorance, tolerate each other, listen to new ideas, and think of 'Truth' as a working hypothesis. Jehovah and Allah and Krishna and Buddha belong in the trash bin of history."

All this happened before June 6, 1944.

Chapter VI

CLEARLY, the 173rd General Hospital had been set up for one purpose—to care for the inevitable huge casualties that would occur when the Allies stormed the beaches of France. On June 6,1944, D-Day arrived. Suddenly the 173rd changed from a leisurely, overstaffed hospital to a chaotic effort of exhausted doctors, nurses, pharmacists, orderlies, ambulance drivers, supply sergeants, cooks, launderers and sterilizers, maintenance men and clerks. The only group not running around frantically was a few officers there to make it "an Army." These officers finally did what the military loathes to do—let people be responsible for themselves. The colonel announced, "I'm sure we all want to do all we can to help our wounded comrades, so I'm asking you to go beyond your assigned shifts, sleep and eat as little as you can, and stay on duty as long as possible."

They all did. The wounded arrived in caravans of ambulances, still wearing dirty combat fatigues, flown in straight from the front. Wards spilled out into corridors, and corridors spilled outside onto walkways. Although the most serious cases were taken first, some still died waiting. Brad knew some he'd worked on would never walk again, some would never see again. He held a white man's black hand that felt like an old leather glove while the doctor cut it off. He hated himself once because, rushing around to the other side of the operating table, he touched a lamp and had to waste time scrubbing again.

Once he had the thrill of having ready a very unusual instrument before the doctor screamed for it. Brad would never forget his first heart operation. You think of surgery involving only subtle, intricate techniques and technology. But to get inside the ribs, the doctor used a branch cutter with two-foot-long handles. He grunted as he crunched down on the rib until a loud crack sprung it in two. Much later in the operation, Brad got a most unusual command—"Take hold of this kelly"(a surgical pliers). The kelly handles were sticking out of the chest. "Pull it out," the doctor said. Brad did. Clasped in the kelly's teeth was a bullet. "Now," said the doctor, "you'll have a great story for your kids—you removed a bullet from a man's heart." The young doctor had not done something quite as stupid as it sounds. The heart is surrounded by a strong cardiac sack. The bullet had penetrated the cardiac sack, but miraculously had not damaged the heart muscle at all. Brad still got a great war story.

Sometimes the tension spilled over the brim. A nurse does not hand a doctor an instrument. She slaps it into his hand, so there's no doubt who has it. One nurse, very angry with a doctor, kept slapping instruments into his hand so hard that later he had blisters. His macho refused to stop her.

A most horrifying event happened one night when Ben, Buck and Brad walked into their Quonset hut at 10:00 PM, weary after fourteen hours in the OR. There on the floor, on his back, crying and pleading, lay this effeminate soldier, Neil. He had often commented about the "big dong" of Dan, a lanky, raw-boned, dumb, ignorant hillbilly. While ten guys watched, Dan had his knees on Neil's arms, pinning him, and was rubbing his penis on Neil's face, shouting, "You keep on talking about it, so suck it! Suck it!" The three Bs managed to pull Dan off. Neil ran out. He was never seen again.

Meanwhile, when it seemed the 173rd could not possibly handle one more soldier, ambulances kept rolling in. Minor matters, flesh wounds, shrapnel in soft tissue, were performed in corridors by flashlight. Some recovering GI's had to sit on benches to free up beds. This lasted for several weeks. But in a few months, France was conquered and hospitals were set up on the continent. The war was winding down. The 173rd returned to a leisurely life. In fact, the Army was stumped for ways to keep men busy. Brad jumped at an amazing offer—a week at Oxford University! The intent was to have young American soldiers form a bond with young British students. What an opportunity! Brad slept in a regular Oxford dorm, put his shoes outside the door at night to be polished, and soaked up this fabled atmosphere. He wandered into a small chapel and lay down on a pew to admire the stained glass windows. Immediately the chapel was filled with Bach's Toccata and Fugue in D minor. Someone practicing the organ. It was the closest Brad had felt to God in a long time.

In the welcoming speech, the droll professor said, "Even when you are out of your room after dark, you must close your blackout curtains. For you see, the chap across the hall might have his lamp on, and the light would shine through his transom, cross the hall, go through your transom, then down out your window, and be of invaluable help to any Nazi pilot flying below your window and looking up."

A professor who had lived thirty years in America and thirty years in England, lectured on the contrast between the two countries. "In many multi-syllable words, Englishmen accent the beginning of the word and Americans accent the end. This is caused by the Brits being so unsure of themselves, that as soon as they hear their voice, they start to trail off; while the Yanks exude such confidence that, hearing their voice, they crescendo to an accent." Every day, Brad feasted on wonderful lectures. He attended a political debate between Lady Astor and a young radical who said, "Of course I have great sympathy for Lady Astor's blasted city." He ate in the wood-paneled dining hall on ancient oak tables. He hungered to be in college. More than the pull of any earthly pleasures, this craving for knowledge would become the real enemy of his theology.

He wrote to Kay at great length about all of this, pouring out to her the troubles of his mind: "The more I read what the best minds have discovered about this tiny world and huge universe of ours, the more childish the Bible seems. I try to tell myself that the ultimate truth is simple and pure like a child, that Jesus' love washes away all the doubts created by science. But then the silly picture of God making the earth first, then hanging lights in the sky, stands next to the overwhelming evidence of a universe billions of years older than the earth, the earth spinning its wheels billions of years before man, and man stumbling around a million years before he could hardly talk. Our sun is a very ordinary star, and there are more stars than all the grains of sand on earth! Why would God create all that if we were his only real goal? I don't know what to think. I do know how I feel—I feel my faith slowly slipping away with each book I read, with each mental wrestling match with Ben. God forgive me! As Pope wrote:

> Sole judge of truth, in endless error hurled,
> the glory, jest and riddle of the world, and Hood

wrote:
> I remember, I remember fir trees dark and high,
> I used to think their tender tops
> were close against the sky.
> It was a childish ignorance, but now it's little joy

to know I'm farther off from Heaven
than when I was a boy

This time Brad did not end his letter with a love poem, but
with this:

In the beginning there was darkness
upon the face of Heaven. And man saw
the darkness and was afraid.
Man said, "Let there be God!"
and there was God. Men stood in awe.
Men saw poetry on their faces
and knew that God was good.
Rulers saw they could pick the pockets
of men with their arms raised in prayer,
so rulers said God could stay.
After a while, the arms of men
grew tired holding up the fingers' smile
toward God. Hands drizzled into
pockets—empty pockets.
Man saw sullen prose
on the faces of men.
Poetry—minor poems—was left
to rulers waiting trial.
Zarathustra left his mountain watch
to tell man God was dead.
Man sighed and said,
"All right,
let there be light."

Kay wrote back, as always, comforting him: "I would be
the last person to give good advice on what you are struggling
with. I don't feel at all at home with religion or science or
philosophy. But God can hardly blame you for thinking, if
that's the kind of brain he created. You go ahead and figure

out what ideas are best for you, and let God worry about how he likes it."

So Brad was no longer an overly mature twelve-year-old child, no longer a religiously inspired eighteen-year-old youth, but a complex twenty-two-year-old man.

Brad felt he had to start his next letter to Kay with a love poem:

> My love for you makes metaphors
> from all there is—
> lawns and their mowers,
> loans and their owers,
> snow, for instance:
> snow simplifies, unshapes the earth,
> cancels city curbs and country stones.
> samely colors and textures
> town cement and virgin ground.
> Just so,
> my love for you
> smooths, connects and whitens all I know.

He continued his letter:

> I recently read Dostoevsky's *Brothers Karamazov*, in which there is a long dream about Jesus coming back to earth and clashing silently with the Church. That night I had a dream where I was the Devil and God confronted me for having gone to earth and shown Adam and Eve the tree of knowledge. Enclosed is a literary version of my dream:
>
> The Devil stood there, a mixture of contrition and defiance, waiting for God. God entered, a perfect picture of a patriarch, white-headed, white-bearded, a burdened smile on his wizened face. Short steps bring his bent body to his throne. He speaks. "My

advisers say I should string you up. Should I? What do you have to say for yourself?"

"Oh God," the Devil says, "if living with the pains of ignorance isn't torture enough, then torture me some more, but for my soul's sake, tell me why knowledge is evil. Tell me why I was made to strain for light, when I'm locked in a room with thick iron shutters on the windows. Is it my fault I'm not like the other angels whose brains are asleep. Dark rooms are fine for sleeping, but you don't know what it's like to be awake in a dark room, to see the window and shutters and know there's light beyond." God looks at the Devil with a sad "don't I?" expression. With an amazed, hoarse whisper the Devil moans, "No. Yes. You do know how it feels. Even you don't know the answer. There is no answer. Heaven is an ignorant pyramid of authority, pointing to you for justification, and you are a bluff."

Calmly, God replies, "You have done enough and said enough for hanging. If I spare the rope, there's no special pity for you. My love is always constant and infinite for every soul in Heaven. It has grown to be a dispassionate passion. You have done a vile thing, perhaps vile enough to shake the Kingdom of Heaven. If lynching you could stop the tremors, my best official smile would broaden while the rope raised you. These sound like words of hate. But I have forgotten how to hate. I rule. As a ruler, I think it would be unwise to make a martyr out of you. You were forbidden to go down to earth, so I cannot turn you loose to become an example of defiance. Let me try to convince you not to defy me."

"I wanted," the Devil says, "to besiege your castle and capture your Absolute Truth, but now you admit it doesn't exist. The joy of my defiance is gone.

Yet I must continue to fight against this shameful sham."

God says, "Usually I speak briefly. Often not at all. Now I must tell you the long story. In the beginning—and perhaps there was no beginning— there was..."

The Devil interrupts, "What do you mean— perhaps there was no beginning?"

God continues, "Angels slowly became conscious of themselves and the universe. What went before, no one knows. In the beginning, there was no God." The Devil asks, "You have not always existed?"

"No," God answers, "I was a latecomer. It took them a long time to make a God. First they had to struggle for life itself. Death was not then, like now, an invited guest—he broke down the door. Slowly they conquered disease and death, and built the simple beauties and complicated gadgets we have today. This was the first big battle—angels against death. And the angels won. The second big battle was angels against angels. The problem was, to use a homely idiom, now that the cake was baked, who was going to eat it. Everyone had a different idea on how to cut the cake. The angels who made the recipe wanted the knife. The angels who owned the flour wanted the knife. The yeast angels rose up. All those who fired the ovens and cleaned the pans decided they didn't need a knife and stormed the bakeries with their fingers foremost. Groups formed with flags and slogans and armies. The battle lasted a long time. We almost wiped ourselves out. Slowly something became clear: after all, it was a pretty big cake, and we could bake more. Maybe we just liked to fuss and feud, and maybe some of the leaders would rather fight than eat. So slowly we picked out the good ideas and threw out the bad leaders. We used our feuding energies for the third and last battle: angels searching for the Ultimate Truth. Our brains, not our brawn, had won the first and second battles. As disease and social unrest became minor problems, latecomers, like myself, turned our thinking to the universe. What was it? Why was it? Was it a toy of some Superior Being or was it a horseless carriage, driverless too, running, but not running anywhere? We had the tools to look inside atoms and outside of Heaven. We pried into protons and stared at stars."

The Devil exclaims, "What an exciting age !"

"Yes," God says, "exciting for the few of us whose brains were too big, but bewildering and divisive for angels in general. We seemed like microbes on a speck of cosmic dust. For all we knew, what we called the universe might merely be molecules of water in a glass in a giant's hand. In a moment, he'd grow thirsty and down we'd go. There was no good reason to believe such silliness, but no proof to doubt it. Angels argued about supernatural possibilities and pledged devotion without any evidence. We had lost the battle for knowledge."

"You mean you quit?"

"Yes," God said, "I knew you'd use that word for it—we quit. We hunted for hundreds of centuries, and when we did not know where else to look, we still kept on looking. And in spite of the uncertainty which seeped into every angel's soul, we kept on looking! Then, when we saw they began to doubt the value of everything, began to lose respect for each other and for life itself, when we saw the battle of angel against angel would start again, we quit! Then the wisest among us said, 'Let there be God.' And I, who loved the search for Truth the most—I, who least wanted to quit— I was chosen to be God. On punishment of death, no angel could mention me or regard me as anything but the Supreme Being of the Universe, the source of Infinite Wisdom and Infinite Love. This all happened long ago. All the angels who were alive then, except me, have long since grown tired of living and are now dead. These events, these seeds of doubt, survive only in the dim unconscious memory of the race. Heaven has a sound Faith, and it has become a better place since we stopped stumbling after unattainable Truth. I have truly become God. No longer am I merely a benevolent dictator; I am the Divine Authority. Angels being what they are, no juster Heaven is possible. The theoretical absurdity of my position is no longer painful or even humorous to me. It is part of my Infinite Wisdom. I have had only one fear—that someday you would float up out of the unconscious memory of the race. Now you are here. I have told you what you came to find out. Do you want to be a martyr for this teasing temptress, Truth, and perhaps lead Heaven back down the destructive road of doubt?"

The Devil asks, "Why was *I* made to ask questions if there are no answers?"

God answers, "There are many answers. You ask the wrong questions."

"If my questions are evil, why is my guilt not strong enough?" the Devil pleads. "Why can I not make peace with good and evil until I have the knowledge of good and evil?"

God calmly answers, "Because you are sinful, the Incarnation of Sin. In the psychologist's language, you must learn to repress and sublimate. In my language, your soul must seek salvation. Don't yield to the thrill of being different. You are not new. Heaven went through all this long ago. You're a page from a burnt history book. There is nothing out there we can know or need to know. What you see as a grandiose search for truth is really the most sinful sort of idle curiosity. Heaven has important questions. Help us find those answers. For instance, we became a classless society ages ago, yet there are still some class animosities. How can we root out ill will between large groups or small families? Such questions are not as big as the universe, but they are more important."

"Dear God," the Devil says warmly, "you are good. But I cannot kneel to that kind of goodness. You destroyed history."

"Weren't you listening?" God demands. "It was no whim, no power-mad censorship, no burying big truths which we did not want others to know. We buried our ignorance and sowed the seeds of Faith."

The Devil insists, "Our ignorance is a big truth everyone should know."

God insists, "They did know, and they felt like frightened fish in a fathomless ocean."

The Devil smiles. "You choose analogies from earth."

God frowns. "Oh, earth. I love earth. I had hoped it would be better than Heaven."

The Devil offers, "Perhaps it will be, if people seek knowledge."

"Knowledge failed!"God shouts. "Faith has succeeded. Angels no longer feel like future fossils. They are the divine court of God, the center of the universe. Stars are just jewels for their ceilings, not separate suns, and the sun is only a central heating system. We no longer worry about mapping the Milky Way, we..."

The Devil interrupts, "Did you map it?"

"Of course," God answers. "We wandered around in the stars. Space exploration, we called it then, but it turned out to be wandering."

"You found nothing interesting out there?" the Devil asks.

"It was all interesting, very interesting," God answers. "But nothing out there hinted what the universe is, and nothing from there helped Heaven. Sooner or later—no, it was shamefully later—we saw how sinful our idle curiosity was. Then you sneak down to earth to tempt them with the fruit of knowledge, the bitter fruit, the old mistake, so old we had forgotten. What an unoriginal sin yours is."

"You've tried to fill in a volcano."

"We have filled it in!"

"It will erupt!"

"No, some rumblings way down, but no eruption."

"I have erupted."

God laughs gently, "You're not really molten. You're a cold stone and can be cast out of Heaven. You are a single weed, easily plucked out of the garden. I shall not make a martyr out of you. You will leave Heaven at once. No one, not even the Archangels, will know what became of you. No one in Heaven will ever mention you again. Now you can go get drunk on freedom. Go waste yourself on an eternal trip to nowhere. Go find out that all except Heaven is Hell. Go and see how long you can kid yourself that you are on a worthy search for knowledge."

"And if I find it?"

"If you find it, come home a hero! You suspect

me, don't you? You think I'd rather not know, so I can go on playing God. No, my eyes are as eager as yours to see beyond blind faith. But I've looked, and I know those are more blessed who have not seen and believe."

The Devil asks, "I can go to earth?"

God answers sadly, "Oh, earth! You were to be a paradise! I found a race being born, a new race which did not have you hidden in its memory. They were to learn only love. Instead of work, worship. You suspect me again, don't you? I did not need their worship. They needed to worship me. You've ruined them. Their race is on its way to repeat all our follies. Yes, go to earth. It's more yours now than mine."

The Devil is close to tears. "I do not suspect you of anything but goodness. You have shared your wisdom with me and I am grateful, even though you have almost killed all of my hope. Yet I am either too strongly stupid or too weakly moral to live with your lie. Forgive me, dear God, I cannot repent."

Chapter VII

*I*N April, 1945, disease killed Roosevelt and his own gun killed Hitler. America had elected FDR four times. Harry S. Truman would serve out the remaining three years, a lightweight politician of dubious qualifications, a product of a corrupt Missouri machine. Derisively referred to as "Hairy Ass Truman," Truman turned out to be one of America's best presidents.

After Germany fell in May, 1945, the Allies anticipated at least a year or two of fighting Japan, island by island with many casualties. But by August, 1945, the United States had learned how to break the unbreakable atom, this tiniest indestructible piece of anything, releasing the enormous force that held the atom together. America dropped an atomic bomb with the explosive power of twenty thousand tons of TNT on Hiroshima. Three days later, America exploded an even more powerful bomb on Nagasaki, and Japan surrendered.

Releasing 17 million men from the armed forces took time. Brad did not get discharged until May,1946. Seventeen million men of working age, suddenly thrown on the labor market, created a huge problem, especially as war production would be drastically reduced. One smart thing the government did to lower the pressure for jobs was the GI Bill—a totally free college education: tuition, books, room and board and even pocket money. This not only helped the labor problem, but became a national treasure, creating an enormous educated class. From then on, ordinary people considered college a normal goal. Brad jumped at the chance, enrolling at Stanford University, partly to go to the other coast, mainly for their prestigious philosophy department.

During the summer, Brad and Dex and other high school buddies enjoyed a wonderful vacation at the "Fifty-two Twenty Club." The government set up this club for returning veterans. For fifty-two weeks, you could go every Friday morning to this office. They would ask, "Have you found a job?" You would answer, "No." They would ask, "Are you looking for a job?" You would answer, "Yes." They would give you twenty dollars, not a small amount because, like the old joke of George Washington being able to throw a silver dollar across the Potomac, a dollar went much farther in those days.

Each of these young men were two different men at the same time. They had gone to school together for twelve years, then had not seen each other for four years. Now here they were again on the same streets, the same softball fields, the same hamburger joints. It felt like the summer after high school. There was also that other person who had been through a war, who was twenty-three, not nineteen, but he had done that with totally different people in other strange places. That war veteran continually intruded at moments when Brad would say, "Let's go find Ed," and the answer would be, "He's dead. Anzio Beach." Brad stood for a long time in front of City Hall, looking incredulously at the plaque. It listed eighty-three men from his small city killed in the war. He had known half of them. Several had been friends.

But the vacationers had a glorious summer. They bought and sold and swapped cars in a wild used-car market, as there were no new ones yet. Brad reverted to the wheels he had at the end of high school, a motorcycle. They spent long days at the ocean, turning Jersey sand into castles, body surfing waves, throwing a football, intuitively shying away from burying each other. They reminisced about school days, avoiding war stories to keep that adult person away. Brad, who had been writing a lot of poetry, was easily persuaded to read some as the gang settled down near sunset after a tiring day. He kept it light:

> A firefly, the first this year.
> It says in long-drawn trochees,
> "Summer, summer, summer's here."

and

> Giggling girls with wiggling curls
> were walking down the street.
> Whistling guys with bristling thighs
> were talking indiscreet.
>
> Hacked, bland hags with black handbags
> sneered that it was outrageous.
> Eye-glassed men with bypassed yen
> feared that it was contagious.

Around an evening beach fire, Dex said, "Hey, Mary, did we ever tell you about the time Brad's arm almost fell off?"

"No."

"Well, we were in Brad's apartment, drinking Cokes, and Dave took Ed into the kitchen, supposedly to tell him a secret. I said to Brad, 'We're playing a trick on Ed. Get a broom.' He did. I got on a chair and held a glass of Coke against the ceiling and told Brad to hold the broom handle under the glass. He did, with a big grin, anticipating the fun. Then Dave and Ed came back. We sat down and talked, and Brad suddenly realized what was going on. Now that glass of Coke was right over the middle of his dad's cherished oriental rug. Soon Brad was pleading, 'Come on, guys, my arm is falling off!' Finally Ed took pity and got on a chair to hold the Coke."

Mary said, "I wish Ed were here."

Dave quickly drove the adult intruders away, asking, "Brad, why didn't you stay and play poker with us last night?"

With a troubled brow, Brad answered, "I couldn't believe the way you guys were betting—a dollar to open, two dollars to raise. Good God, you could lose hundreds!"

"Yeah, I did. Carl lost his car."

"Mary," Brad said, "I remember one snowy afternoon at Dave's house, playing penny ante. Dave had a great hand, but ran out of pennies. So he rushed into the kitchen and came back with six empty milk bottles, each worth five cents as a deposit refund. We were all glad he won, because nobody wanted to slosh home with those bottles."

Why the heavy gambling? Perhaps as a replacement for the exciting combat of war. Perhaps because they had risked their lives and needed another big risk. Perhaps they hated thinking about joining the responsible adult world where money matters.

Of course, the best part of this vacation for Brad was Kay. He was no longer a premature twelve-year-old, but a mature young man. Kay was well into her thirties, and while she did not look "getting on," she no longer looked girlish. The slight wrinkles added an interesting complexity without in any way diminishing the vivacious, teasing, yet always sympathetic smile. Brad adored this ripened woman. They enjoyed the long history and shared memories of their affair. They were old friends as well as still passionate lovers.

Now that Brad was a "man," Kay's mother was adamant that he could not stay in their house. Dave's parents owned a big hotel, and Brad rented a room for almost nothing. This turned out to be the best arrangement, as Kay could come and go as she pleased, and she came a lot. They would lie in bed together, long after their passion passed, gently caressing and talking, sometimes quite seriously. She asked, "How are you getting along with God these days?"

He almost cried and answered, "I've lost him. I miss him so much. You don't know how happy I felt, feeling close to the Creator, how proud to follow Jesus. Now it's all gone. I know what Thomas Hood meant when he wrote, 'I remember, I remember fur trees dark and high. I used to think their tender tops were close against the sky. It was a childish ignorance, but now it's little joy to know I'm farther off from heaven than when I was a boy.'"

Kay asked, "So what do you believe now?"

"Nothing. I mean, nothing cosmological. My guess is that we have no connection with this vast universe except our tiny time on this tiny planet."

"Well," Kay said, "you might be farther off from heaven, but you're much closer to me than when you were a boy. Stay. Don't go to California. Stay here and write poetry. I'll help support you."

He was amazed. "Wow! I can't believe you said that. I'm so flattered. You really love me that much?"

"That much."

"You know I can't. Not because I don't love you. You know I do. I've loved you since before I knew what love was. But I've got to go to college and find out what the wise men thought, and maybe even find some live wise men."

"Why can't you go someplace close—Columbia or Princeton?"

"Because I'd wear out my motorcycle rushing to see you. I want to plunge into learning. I want to wear out a chair in the library. I want to buttonhole a professor after class and make him pour more knowledge into me."

"You'll also meet sparkling, beautiful young women, and

you'll fall in love, and I'll be a distant memory."

"Kay darling, no matter what casual encounters I have with other females, you will always own my heart."

She tried unsuccessfully to believe him. He straddled his old Harley and rode to Stanford University, California.

Chapter VIII

*B*RAD'S college goals were very clear. While he loved poetry second only to philosophy, he would not take literature courses. He had just spent three years in the Army devouring literature, so he wanted to use professors where he needed them most—math, science, French and, of course, philosophy. He planned to graduate in three years, studying two summers.

His professors thrilled Brad. In philosophy, Professor Markovsky probed for truth with his thick Slavic accent through a cloud of smoke which came from the cigarette held dead center between his lips while he spoke. The ash would get longer and longer, then fall on his lapel. At that point, he would take the cigarette from his mouth to flick off the ashes, notice they were on his lapel, make an ineffectual attempt to brush them off, put the butt back in his mouth, and the process would begin again. He died of lung cancer a year later.

For math, Professor Hotchkiss was a roly-poly, buoyant, bouncy man whose jacket was always too tight. With a devilish grin, he would ask, "Ah, but what happens when X is greater than Y?" and rush to the blackboard, furiously write equations as if racing someone, then turn to the class with a triumphant, high-pitched laugh.

The science professor was a vivacious woman only three years older than Brad, with flowing, flaming red hair. She formed a chemical bond with the veterans in her class.

French class often resembled a football cheering squad, to cement the pronoun order: *"Me le, me la, me les , te le, te la, te les, le luil la lui, les lui!!"* Of course, Brad acquired the indispensable knowledge that *"la plume de ma tante est sur le bureau de mon oncle."*

Most memorable was the class when Professor Markovsky, himself a dying man, said, "Tonight, you veel read about da death of Socrates. But I vant da pleasure to tell you part of it. Socrates vas accused of corrupting da youth of Athens through his teaching. Sentence—death. But da law said an accused could offer an alternative punishment. Dey vanted him to propose retirement to countryside. Socrates said, 'I propose as an alterative punishment dat da city of Athens build me a school large enough so I can open the minds of all da young men of Athens.' Your assignment, ven you read dat, is to cry."

Campus life was somewhat strange, as most of the freshmen were veterans, older than most of the seniors. Brad was talking one day with another vet when a young senior approached them and said, "Hey, frosh, you're not wearing your freshmen beanies."

The other vet, who had stormed the beach at Normandy, smiled and replied, "Kid, if you want me to wear that silly hat, why don't you just put one on me?" Thus ended a long tradition.

The campus pleasantly surprised Brad. It was so not like eastern educational institutions, so not Oxford, so California. The red tile roofs, the soft tan stucco walls, the gently arched walkways, all blended perfectly with "the farm." Students called it the farm because it really was one. Mr. Stanford had purchased thousands of acres and stipulated that the campus would be surrounded by working farms. From the high bell tower you could see all the way to San Francisco. Brad grew to love that city of horrible weather and wonderful variety. From the Oakland side, with the Bay covered by the frequent fog, San Fran looked like a city in the sky above the clouds.

The way we say "back east" but "out west" shows the Atlantic orientation of our history. We think thick growths of maple, oak and elm, where you can't see very far even on a rise, is the natural landscape. Out west (except in the mountains which are twice as high as the eastern chain), trees are sparse and low, and the tall palms and eucalyptus have little foliage, so from a slight elevation, you can see forever, with a big sky all around. Brad enjoyed the spacious views.

Of all the thorny philosophical problems Brad struggled with, nothing troubled him as much as free will. "Professor Sophman," he asked, "if Newton was right, that every piece of matter changes only when an outside force moves it, and we are matter, doesn't that mean that I shoot someone, or don't shoot someone, because of all the advising voices that have influenced my neurons, plus my genes and what I had for breakfast? Where is there room for my free will?"

Professor Sophman smiled and said, "Marcus Aurelius, a determinist, was beating his servant one day. The servant protested, 'But master, you know I was predetermined to make that mistake.' Aurelius replied, 'Yes, but it was also predetermined that I would beat you for it.'"

The class laughed. "Of course you laugh,"said the professor. "Such fatalism mocks our most vital convictions— that an effort can be made, that we can judge each other and hold someone accountable. But haven't we always laughed at ridiculous ideas, like the world being round? Fools in high places still laugh at Einstein and Darwin. Determinism is a very rational, consistent philosophy with much supporting evidence. But we have this powerful feeling that we are free to choose, to weigh, to judge, to consider, to decide."

Someone asked, "What do you think is correct?"

He answered by asking, "How many of you have a different religion than both of your parents?" Two hands went up. The professor continued, "And that doesn't prove you made independent decisions, for you could have had unusual forces working on you. I feel sure of this—if we have free will, it is a tiny force, often defeated. Yet that tiny force might get a finger to push a button and send a huge elevator up or down. Let's hope we all know the right direction."

Brad was elated yet troubled by all these exhilarating classes. Could all his struggles into and out of God's embrace have been determined by physical and psychological forces he neither knew of nor had any control over? How much more complicated everything became when you dove deep into metaphysics and ethics. How clear it used to be when there was only God talking through Jesus. But he knew, no matter how strong the yearning, he could not go back. He was now in love with learning and thinking. He now regarded religion as a reformed drug addict looks back on drugs—the desire to get high is still there, but the sober life is the right life.

The beach did not entice Brad. The Jersey shore had the warm Gulf Stream coming up the East Coast to heat the water. California had an Alaska Current coming down the West Coast to shiver swimmers. A special thrill, impossible to see on the Jersey shore, was the sun setting over the ocean. He loved to ride his big old Harley along the Coast Highway, whose curves were carved into the steep cliffs. The only fear he had on his motorcycle was when riding slowly through town. A huge dog, a boxer, would charge out of an alley, barking and snarling, and try to bite Brad's leg. Always a different alley, always when least expected. A frightening scene, with Brad kicking and trying to stay balanced and to get away without running into anything. One day, Brad thought maybe he could teach the boxer to get along with the motorcycle, so just at the point where Brad had escaped and the boxer had stopped, Brad stopped and kept gunning the motor. The dog couldn't resist and came charging. Brad stayed slightly ahead. Whenever the boxer stopped, so did Brad, gunning the motor. They went out on a country road, over five miles. Finally the dog lay down beside the road, panting, watching Brad ride back and forth. Then Brad parked next to his adversary, leaving the motor running. He sat down next to the vanquished and petted him and told him what great friends they'd be from now on. But the next day, the boxer shot out of an alley, snarling and biting at Brad's heels.

Brad's knee would not let him consider going out for football, and he felt even if he had been physically able, he would not want to give so much time to something which once meant everything to him. He had become a scholar. However, he did organize a touch football league, became a member of the student senate and captained the debating team. All this, plus his excellent marks should, he thought, be worth a shot at a Rhodes Scholarship. He applied. He got to the stage where he would be interviewed by a committee of ex-Rhodes Scholars. When he walked into the room and saw, sitting behind a table, five sixtyish men, he felt he was back facing that Draft Board. Things were going well until one corpulent man said, "I notice you don't belong to a fraternity."

"Well, I thought the frat house life would be a distraction from the path I've chosen."

"But the friendships, the camaraderie, the contacts for later on in life," insisted the round one, "are an important part of college life. Some of my dearest friends are old fraternity brothers."

"Well, also," said Brad, who seldom thought of the consequences for expressing his thoughts, "the fraternities ban Jews and Negroes, and I don't think that's right."

The old man pushed on. "But aren't we all entitled to our

own tastes? I don't want to live with Jews and Negroes. I've nothing against them. They're just not my kind. It's like peas. I don't eat peas because I don't like peas. What do you say to that?"

What Brad said next he sometimes thought about years later and was never sure whether or not he regretted it. "I think your mother should have taught you to eat your vegetables." The meeting came to a pretty quick close after that.

Brad had become friends with his French professor, Monsieur Beaujolie. As French basically has no stressed syllables, the French accent in English gives a wonderful smooth flow to our language. But when a Frenchman tries to hit our strong accents, the odds are against him on three or more syllables. Monsieur Beaujolie almost always lost the gamble, giving his fluent English a delightful syncopation. "Brad, what will you be doING afTER graduation?"

"Of course," Brad answered, "I'll go on for a Ph.D. in philosophy. But, you know, I've crammed for three straight years, including summers. And as much as I want to get my doctorate and teach, I feel a little burned out. I'd like to get away for a while."

When M. Beaujolie was just thinking out loud, instead of consciously trying to sound American, he would fall into the typical soothing French accent, where all the syllables have equal length with a slight accent on the final syllable. "I have a very warm place in my heart for a small peasant village in the southern mountains of France, called Chambon-sur-Lignon. These farmers are descendants of the old Huguenots, a little island of Protestants in an ocean of Catholics. While France was occupied by the Nazis, these simple people risked their lives by harboring and hiding hundreds of Jews. I have helped them establish a little private school there, le College Cevenol, run by people with a spirit like yours. How would you like to teach English there for a year?"

The young man immediately shouted, "Yes! Great! Thanks!" Not long after that, Brad strapped on his leather helmet, the kind WWI pilots wore, pulled down his goggles, kick-started the Harley and took off for New York harbor. One stop he could not resist was the Great Salt Lake in Utah. Because of his build, he had a hard time floating, even in salt water. He once won a bet, walking across a pool on the bottom. He had heard that even he could float easily in the Great Salt Lake. And float he did! He actually sat up in the water, as if in a chair. Still smiling from the experience, he dried off and mounted his iron steed. About five miles down the road, he began to feel warm all over. *Funny,* he thought, *I wasn't out in the sun long enough to get burned.* Then he noticed his arms were white. A fine layer of salt covered his entire body. The burning rapidly became very uncomfortable and potentially dangerous. Up ahead was a motel. A bearded old codger was rocking in a rocking chair, puffing on a pipe. "Can I rent a shower?" asked Brad.

"Don't rent showers. Rent rooms," came the reply.

"It's 11:00 AM," explained Brad. "I don't need a room, just a shower."

Still puffing and rocking, the old man repeated, "Don't rent showers. Rent rooms." Like many before him, Brad had to yield. On he rode, up over the Rockies, through a line storm in Nebraska. Sometimes he'd ride close behind a huge truck and coast in neutral, with the suction of the truck pulling him along at sixty mph. Danger seldom shouts loud enough when you're in your twenties. A few times at a truck stop, he hitched a ride, and man and bike caught some sleep in the back of an eighteen-wheeler.

The 4Bs had exchanged Christmas cards with short notes, but had not been together in over three years. Bill and Buck were fairly friendly, studying in the same medical school in Chicago. Ben was teaching in a Chicago suburban high school, but had a wife and young child, so very rarely saw them. With Brad coming through Chicago, they arranged a reunion. Just as Brad and his high school pals after the war saw each other as the day after graduation, so the 4Bs saw themselves back in a hospital in England. But they were now in the real world, in their late twenties. Ben was over thirty, and even more cynical and bitter. Still, they accomplished what reunions are supposed to, laughing themselves silly about ether flame throwers, medicinal alcohol cocktails, laughing gas, Brad's circumcision, officers they hated, warm British beer. A whole day of "Do you remember..." and "Whatever happened to..." Bill did not let them avoid the operating room trick they pulled on him. "You have no idea how much that hurt," he said. "I can still feel the hurt if I think about it." But then Bill broke the awkward silent moment with a smile and said, "I gotta admit, it was one helluva stunt." And they all laughed.

It's not true you can't go home again. It is true you can't stay there.

Chapter IX

KAY was now forty with a teenage daughter. A good
mother, not overbearing, not too lenient, Kay made
sure her daughter took health and homework
seriously. They had fun together and loved to go shopping.
Kay insisted she go to public school, albeit a very good public
school, and Kay was on the PTA board to make sure it stayed
that way.

Before going on to France, Brad spent a week in his
hometown. We have already told what a wonderful time Brad
and Kay had together. He was very avuncular with her
daughter, although seeing them together gave Kay a dream-
like deja vu feeling. When he left, Kay almost shouted, "I'm
going with you!" but instead forced that teasing smile and
said, "Don't get seasick."

It turned out to be a good warning. The ship bobbed like
a cork on the ocean, because the small old tub had, until now,
only cruised the Mediterranean and was trying to tap into the
post-war boom in transatlantic voyages. The insurance
companies did not trust its seaworthiness, so Brad's
motorcycle was one of the few pieces of cargo in its hold.
Without ballast, it sailed on the waves, not through them. The
Italian crew served lots of greasy spaghetti, and Brad was

almost alone in the dining room. It was quite a contrast with his previous Army crossing when he stood in line for hours in a chow line. He had lots of time to study French and write love poems for Kay:

Not just until that sickness of the very self, Death,
has robbed your lips of love's expression.
I shall love you after death
has taken what he can.
I don't mean what was always meant—
two spirits in the garden of the moon,
a Heaven hoped for and unbelieved in;
nor that other meaning, years lived out
knowing you are nowhere on this earth—
that sorrow is too terrorizingly believed
to sadden you with the telling.
I shall love what's left of you
when death has taken the breath and heartbeat
and even the awareness of and answer to
my love. I shall fight with maggots
for the right to use your flesh.
I shall fight my horror and disgust
to force apart your now so willing thighs.
I shall fight iconoclastic joy,
and guard the slandered purity of lust.
When I carry you by night up rock to cave, I
want to feel heavy in heart and hand, none of
the strength of madness.
Make myself moan my lessening lust
as you decay from me.
Forbid myself the dirty thrill of evil
of the cheap macabre horror.
Not crazed, but Ulysses like,
feel I cannot yield so soon a love so great,
and love and lose

until I bruise
myself on bone.

Brad figured he would need some sort of permit to ride his Harley in foreign countries, and was told the Automobile Association of America could issue papers good throughout western Europe. When the AAA told him it would cost fifty-six dollars, he was amazed. That was a lot of money in 1949, especially considering his small bank account. So he trusted that if he landed in France without papers, the French would settle it in their favorite fashion— *"ca s'arrange."* At Le Havre, he stood on the dock and watched with alarm as a huge crane dangled his bike from one rope around the handlebars, lifting it high above the ship and slowly swinging it down onto the ground, like a huge lioness moving a cub with her teeth in the back of its neck. Before riding off, he stood for a long while, looking around, thinking of the GI's who waded onto these beaches, some of whom he had helped recover and some he had watched die.

Finally, he mounted his machine and rode to the exit gate. The guard said, "Bonjour, monsieur, zee AAA paypairs?"

"No," replied Brad, "I don't have any AAA papers."

"But monsieur, you must have zee AAA paypairs."

Brad then said in French, "Look, I know America liberated your country, and you still need the USA for many things. But you are once again an independent country, and certainly the great country of France can arrange for someone to travel in your country without depending on an American company."

Ca alors! All sorts of incredulous people started running around, shouting at each other. After fifteen minutes, a man in a much fancier uniform came out of the office, put a sticker on the license plate and said, One dollar eighty-seven cents."

Voila! Ca s'arrange! Brad was on his way to Paris.

He asked for the cheapest hotel and soon found out why it

was the cheapest. From the narrow, dirty street, you entered a building Hollywood would use as the worst possible prison. Everything was barren and dark. The floor was sticky. The room was eight by ten with an iron cot and a shadeless lamp. The window opened onto a five-foot-square smelly air shaft. The toilet was down the hall, labeled with the British WC (dooblavay say), meaning water closet. Brad opened the door and saw a thirty-inch-square iron room with a foot-high iron barrier to be stepped over to enter. There were two footprints with a hole in the middle. The plan was obvious. When he finished, without thinking, he pulled the chain hanging from the ceiling. He found out why it was called a water closet. A Niagra deluge and he was standing in water up to his ankles. Luckily, he was wearing calf-high waterproof boots. He demanded his money back and found a youth hostel.

For three days, he rode slowly all around Paris, stunned at how much more beautiful it is than the best pictures. One evening he went to Le Lapin Agile, the agile rabbit, a tiny, packed nightspot where they served only cherry brandy, and the entertainment was subtle songs or stories or poems, both sad and funny. One was about two 10-year-olds. In French, the standard word for "you" is "vous." One uses "tu" only with close friends or children. One ten-year-old asks the other, "Can we use 'vous' with each other?"

One evening he heard Wagner at the Paris Opera, with Siegfried sounding almost comical singing in French. One evening he went to a movie. An usherette showed him to his seat, which seemed unnecessary as the theater was nearly empty. She stood by him after he sat down. Confused, he asked her why. She said, *"Un pour boire"*(a tip). Flustered, he gave her a ten-franc note. Evidently it was not enough. She crumpled it up, threw it on the floor and walked away.

The time had come to cruise south, through the gentle green countryside, past centuries-old chateaus, over little bridges crossing little streams which later came together in the Loire River. He rode in and almost immediately out of tiny towns with narrow winding streets and low houses. Everything seemed so small and cozy compared to big America.

Finally he reached Lyons, not far from his final destination. He had just come out of its magnificent cathedral and was standing on the steps, surveying the city. A huge chauffeur-driven limousine suddenly screeched its brakes and made a fast u-turn. A man jumped out and came running up the stairs straight at Brad. He shouted, "Class of '24!" having seen Brad's Stanford T-shirt. He turned out to be the chief honcho in Europe for a giant American firm. After lots of talk about the "farm" and what they were both doing there, the executive said, "I'm on my way to my favorite spot for the weekend. You're coming with me. I'll have you back here Sunday evening. My chauffeur will take care of your bike." So Brad went from his small saddle to the most spacious back seat he had ever been in.

They went to a beautiful lake, lac d'Annecy, about halfway between Lyons and Geneva, only an hour's drive. The tall mountains of the French Alps plunged into the lake. A twelfth-century monastery had been converted into a luxurious hotel. The French doors of Brad's room opened onto a veranda from which you could jump right into the lake. The dining room had been the wine cellar, with massive stone walls and low archways. Not one of the many dinner courses had Brad ever seen or tasted or even heard of before, and all delighted his taste buds. "Now, my friend," said the important man, "you are about to taste the best cognac in the entire world, which you can only get here in this ancient abbey." This proved to be the only unpleasant part of a wonderful weekend. Brad hated the taste of strong liquor. He even disliked beer and wine. The most he enjoyed was a slightly spiked sweet drink. Luckily, the glass was small and Brad felt obliged to make believe he enjoyed this medicine. A half hour later, Brad managed to get the last sip down. The host said, "Oh, you're empty," and insisted on another round.

What an introduction to France, he thought, as he rode his bike up onto the high plateau, known as the "massif central," to the west of the Rhone River valley. A narrow country road led him to Chambon-sur-Lignon.

Chapter X

*T*HE town center was one short block, with a grocery store, a hardware store, a storefront room for the one policeman and one postman, a little church, and a bathhouse—twenty-five cents for a shower, fifty cents for a tub. Five side streets had houses. One street led up the hill to the College Cevenol. Besides the surrounding farms, the only business was a lumber mill to take advantage of the many miles of forest all around. The only tall building was a narrow four-story apartment house, one 3-room flat on each floor. It had been arranged for Brad to rent the top floor.

His home consisted of a tiny unheated living room, which he used mostly as a refrigerator; a bedroom with just enough room for the bed and a dresser; a three-foot by three-foot toilet room with no sink; and a fair-sized kitchen containing a table and two chairs, an iron sink with cold running water, and a cast-iron wood-burning stove, the only source of heat in the apartment. The stove reminded him of the stove in his Quonset hut during the war, but he decided against the lighter fluid technique to start it. Instead, he gathered a closet full of shavings from the lumber yard, which made excellent kindling. This would certainly have been against the fire code if the town had had a fire code.

Because of all the dairy farms, flies were always everywhere. No one had screens. He was invited to a fellow teacher's home for tea, and the wife served raisin cake. He surreptitiously waved at the cake, and when the raisins stopped moving, he took a bite. The local population made one concession to combating the flies. They had large screen boxes with a hook in the middle for hanging meat, thus letting the air in and keeping the flies out. Brad persuaded the hardware store owner to sell him a roll of screening. The whole town turned out to watch the crazy American nail screening onto his kitchen window just to banish flies. They told him it would spoil the view, and that was partly true. Being on a high plateau and a fourth floor, he could look across the Rhone Valley to the French Alps. Often a mist hung in the valley and the Alps seemed to float in the sky, just as San Francisco does with fog on the Bay.

One other habit of Brad struck the locals as strange. He bought a liter of milk every day just for himself. Stranger still, he boiled it. Here's why: Every morning the *laiteresse*, a big dirty woman smelling like a cow, would lead her horse and wagon into the town center, ringing her bell and shouting, *"Allez, allez, monsieurs, mesdames, allez, allez!"* People would line up, holding their little milk cans. She would take down from the wagon a huge milk pail, take your can and fill it with a ladle. To make sure she was giving you your money's worth and not wasting any milk, she would hold your can over her pail and fill it until the milk overflowed over her hand and back into the pail. She would give you your can, swipe her hand under her ever-running nose, and take the next can. The milk was also not pasteurized. Brad boiled his milk.

Food was fun. Cabbage was plentiful and once Brad had a yen for the great Irish combo. He hoped the grocer had something resembling corned beef. He explained it at great length to the puzzled grocer, who finally took a guess—*"Ah, peut-etre vous voulez du corned beef.*" Another surprise was asking for a jar of mayonnaise. The grocer sneered, "No Frenchman would let anyone make his mayonnaise for him." Brad took the challenge of beating egg yolks and adding oil drop by drop while beating. You got mayonnaise unless you added some oil too quickly, in which case you suddenly got a layer of egg and a layer of oil, and started all over again.

He taught twelve-year-olds and the seniors, sixteen-year-olds. He loved it. With the youngsters, he shared time-honored American kids' jokes, like "What has four wheels and flies?" (an opportunity to show a verb-noun joke). And it was the perfect chance to tell the one about the American boy who tried to impress his girlfriend with *"Je t'adore,"* but she replied, "Shut it yourself. You left it open." *The kids countered with "Il y a deux grandes choses dans le ciel—l'une, et l'autre est le soleil."* Brad had them read "The Ransom of Red Chief" and "The Lady or the Tiger." The kids always pulled the following trick on foreigners: One would say, *"Monsieur, s'il vous plait, repetez"* and they would all laugh. Brad finally found out that without the "ay" sound, it did not mean repeat, but "fart again."

With the seniors, he offered more serious stuff —*Moby Dick, Death of a Salesman, The Ancient Mariner*. The sharpness and diligence of these students astounded Brad. France started to weed kids out around the age of ten. The less studious were steered to farms and factories. Smart youngsters got a free education right through the university. They took exams much harder than our SAT's at age sixteen. Only a small percentage passed and went on.

So many of these children were beautiful internally, like Jean Pierre. All the students lived in large homes, called *pensions*. This ten-year-old boy had to leave school early in the year. He knew his pension was moving to a new building in April. When they rolled up the living room rug, they found a letter he had left under the rug, saying he knew they would find it when they moved and his love would be with them.

Every chance Brad got—weekends, vacations—he grabbed his sleeping bag, hopped on his Harley and took off. He had sung the French folk song in French class *"sur le pont D'Avignon, on y dance, on y dance."* When he got to Avignon, he found that they had only half finished a bridge across the river, so it was only a large pier, and he sang and danced on it. An unpleasant event occurred there. Brad popped into a *boulangerie* for a typical French lunch—a baguette and a bar of chocolate. France was one-fourth Communist at that time, and the Korean War had just begun. The baker almost punched this American, but his wife knew that business was more important than politics, and Brad got out with his bread and body intact.

Swaying side to side on the winding roads of the Alps, looking up at the Jungfrau and the Matterhorn was reason enough to travel by motorcycle. Of course, he always had the same fun at a border about not having "triple A papers." He entered Italy from the Alps. When Brad told the border guard he was leaving Italy by the Mediterranean coast, the guard said, "OK, I'll give you a paper, but don't come out this way! I don't want this paper back!"

So he coasted down into the lush Po Valley. One night, sleeping in an olive grove, he was awakened at 3:00 AM by men walking along the road singing. In harmony! He recalled a wartime moment, the Welsh coal miners singing on their way home from work, so different from the UMW.

One regret in Rome resulted from Easter. All the images of Jesus were covered for Holy Week, so he only saw a drape where he wanted to see Michelangelo's *Pieta*. He wrote an Easter poem:

> Give us back Easter, you theistic thieves!
> You robbed our Winter Solstice

to fake the unknown birth
of Jesus a date
(scholars say June),
You even kept the Goddess' name—
Easter, she who sang the song of spring
to celebrate the equinox.
Because of Passover
you got the date right.
We'll even grant that dead Jesus
coming back to life
fits in with spring.
But holding out hope for Heaven
defiles the truth of life.
Flowers are enough.

Brad was amazed when, standing inside the Saint Peter's Cathedral, everyone began shouting, *"Papa, Papa,"* and the Pope entered, carried high in a wheel-less carriage by many men. The rowdy, boisterous atmosphere resembled a football stadium more than a church. Nuns lifted small children on their shoulders to see the Pope, and so did Brad.

Brad benefitted by being in Rome for Easter because he heard about an unusual service at a Russian Orthodox Church. Saturday night the congregation gathered to mourn the crucifixion of Jesus. By 10:00 PM, the church was full. Sad music accompanied the condolences exchanged among the mourners. The priest spoke in anguish about the cruelties inflicted on the Son of God and the final indignity of being nailed to a cross like a common criminal. At midnight, the priest said, "Let us go and honor his grave." He led half of the grieving worshipers out of the church. Ten minutes later, they burst back into the church, radiant with joy, shouting, *"Hristos voskress! Hristos voskress!"*(Christ has risen). They rushed around, spreading the news to those who had remained behind. Joy and laughter raced through the crowd.

They hugged and danced and sang praises to God. They made their way into an adjoining huge hall where an enormous feast awaited them. They celebrated until dawn. Brad both smiled and wept at the wonderful ceremony. The smile was for their happiness in having found again their Savior. The tears were for his lost God, gone forever, never to be resurrected.

Brad rode on up the cote d'azur and purposely unrolled his sleeping bag on the beach at Viareggio. Shelley had drowned in the Mediterranean. His body had washed up onto that beach. Italian law, at that time, for health reasons, stipulated that such a body must be burned and buried at that spot. Brad spent an all-night homage to Shelley, remembering as much of his poetry as he could. Although the exact spot of his burial was not known ("the lone and level sands stretched far away"), Brad sensed him under him. Actually, these famous Riviera beaches are not sand but foot-bruising narrow strips of pebbles, laughable compared to the huge sandy shores of America's coasts.

Back in the wood-fired warmth of his kitchen, he wrote more and more poetry, much of it love poems to Kay.

> Love where the roses are?
> under the ground,
> under some cold February star,
> waiting till your sun-smiles
> soften the earth and pour
> the juice of kisses into my winter.
>
> Love where the roots are,
> more than patient, more than faithful,
> a certainty that something not understood
> will push them through the strength of wood
> into a face
> of scented symmetry

in a place
of air and light
where eye and nostril will delight
to find them there.

Just so, you soften the harshest hardness
of the leftover beast in me,
and harden the unformed softness
and turn this gritty chunk of ground
into a garden.

Kay's return comments were always kind, encouraging and grateful, yet also critically astute.

Brad led an intense social life, automatically exotic, speaking French in France with Frenchmen. He had the luxury of breaking into English when stymied, as all the teachers spoke it. He shared long talks with his students out of class. He offered his ideas, and they revealed their young lives, so different from his own youth. He enjoyed the variety on the faculty. Most were as young as him, but ranged from studious, introverted men to flashy, flirty women to studious, introverted women to flashy, flirty men. Janine, one of the wilder women, said to Brad, "You Americans all play bridge, *n'est pas?*"

"It is played a lot in the States," he answered.

"I'd do anything to learn it," she said.

"Anything?"

"Yes. Will you teach me? I'll come to your place Friday night. *D'accord?*"

He quickly said, *"Bien sur."* Now the problem was that the only thing he knew about bridge was that you yelled at your partner, but the offer was too good to pass up. It was already Wednesday. For two days he steered every converson to bridge, and finally found a tutor. On Friday night, Janine learned the game and generously expressed her gratitude.

The affair was casual yet very friendly, with motorcycle picnics and going to parties together. A few years later, Janine visited New York when Brad was living there, teaching by day and writing poetry by night. He wanted to give her a taste of real Americana, so he took her on the subway to Brooklyn, to Ebbets Field, to see the Dodgers play baseball. During the ride, he explained in French how the game was played. The other strap-hangers, avid fans, could not understand French, but they knew from his simulated swings and throws and catches what he was saying. Baseball in French! Sacrilege! Unpatriotic! They were all on their way to see their beloved Dodgers, and hoped the beer and hot dogs would clear away this bad taste. When they arrived at that hallowed stop, a man in front of them turned and said, "Don't forget to tell her what happens when it rains." Janine understood and got all excited—"Tell me! *Dites-moi!* Tell me!" Brad told her.

One older man at the College Cevenol, Phillip Detruit, was wilder than any of the younger teachers. One day the history teacher had tied his tie so that the back part was longer than the front part. While he was lecturing, Detruit walked into his class with scissors, cut the back part even, and walked out. Another time, he strode angrily into the faculty room, shouting, "It's freezing in here! Keep the goddam window closed!" The window opened outward, and he slammed it shut. Shattered glass flew everywhere, and he marched out. Then the puzzled teachers noticed that the window was intact. Detruit had brought a pane of glass in with him under his coat and dropped it as he slammed the window shut.

Not all was cheerfully bucolic in this country village. The only doctor in town rented a house from a morose drunk, who hated and badgered the doctor. One morning, the drunken landlord pounded on the front door, yelling, "You— doctor! Great wise doctor! Out! Out of my house! I don't want you one more minute in my house!" All the while pounding on the door's window.

The doctor appeared at the top of the stairs and shouted, "It's my house until my lease is up. Now go home and sleep it off," and went back into his bedroom.

"Listen, you high and mighty bastard," yelled the landlord, "get out of my house right now or I'll break down the door and throw you out!"

The doctor reappeared at the top of the stairs with a shotgun. "You listen, old man, if you break in, I will shoot you dead!" The landlord picked up a rock, broke the pane, reached in and threw back the bolt and stormed in. The blast blew him back out the door with nine pellets in his chest. There was a perfunctory investigation, no trial, and the doctor calmly saw his patients that afternoon.

Brad got an inside look at how the local farm families lived, because he had done one a small favor. They had a cousin in America who did not speak French, so they asked Brad to translate a letter. They insisted he come to dinner. When he arrived, he sensed some confusion. One member disappeared and dinner was delayed until he returned. Later Brad learned that a guest brings wine, and they did not have enough without his bottle, so someone had to rush out to the store. The one-story house had been built by piling up local rocks for walls two feet thick, with mud packed between them. The floor was dirt, as smooth and hard and even as cement. The ceiling was the thatched roof, held up by huge, hand-hewn rafters. The massive table and chairs were also handmade, rustic but very comfortable. Light came from candelabres. Apparently, there was no gas or electricity. A large fireplace provided the only, but adequate, heat.

Finally they sat down to eat. They surprised Brad by serving on very nice dinnerware. First came appetizers of smoked fish, olives, breaded onion rings, and pickled asparagus, artistically arranged. Then came a thick barley soup, magnificently flavored with all sorts of wonderful, unidentifiable things floating in it. Next came the salade course with red, white, orange, yellow and green vegetables in a seasoned mustard, oil and vinegar dressing, accompanied by crisp, hot bread. Brad left enough room for what he thought was the main course, a cauliflower and bacon dish in a creamy cheese sauce. But he soon discovered that was only the vegetable course! Steak and baked potato arrived, and he really stuffed. And of course, no one ever refuses a perfect chocolate cake! He did have to fake eating the final course— cheese and fruit. The strong coffee at last signified the end of the meal. Peasant life wasn't really so bad.

All too soon, it seemed, the students stood up, as was the French custom, for the last time when Brad entered the classroom. He boiled his last liter of milk, looked out on the Loire Valley through his homemade screen one last time, and pointed his Harley toward Le Havre.

Chapter XI

*A*s eagerly as Brad always anticipated seeing Kay again, never so much as now. She was the one constant among all the variables in his life. Thinking about his sexperiences, only with Kay did the term "making love" seem appropriate for "having sex." Driving along, Even his hometown seemed strange. While the buildings had not changed, the population, almost all white before the war, was now almost all black. Newark had branched out into the suburbs. As he passed the candy store where, as a thoughtless child, he had bought "nigger babies," he felt sure they did not sell THEM anymore. His friends, who were able to pretend after the war that they were still high school kids at the beach, were now trapped or liberated in adulthood. Dex, married, worked on Wall Street with his father. Dave had a kid. Mary had two. Carl still gambled, but with stocks, not cards. Ah, but Kay, Kay was still warm and winking, sexy in every cell of her body without trying. We have already told what a wonderful week of loving they had together, as always so pheromoniously matched, before he kicked down on the starter arm and retraced the route to California.

As planned, he stopped off in Reno for a month to make some money. Not gambling, of course, but as a busboy in a high-class hotel. In the 1950s, Reno was the Las Vegas of its day. Men drifted in and out. Jobs were quickly available. Gambling conquered every place and every person. In the grocery store, at the end of the checkout counter, slot machines waited to gobble up your change. Unskilled workers were paid twice a week so they would not go hungry more than a few days. Brad scooped up dirty dishes in a very expensive restaurant. The French chef earned so much that he had a chauffeur-driven Rolls Royce. This culinary master's office was near the kitchen's exit. He happened to look out one evening as Brad passed. Brad complimented him on the evening's delicious chocolate-raspberry cake—in French. The chef beamed with pleasure, not for the compliment, but to hear French. He pulled Brad into his office for a long talk about his beloved homeland. After that, he often called Brad in to sample a goody and chat in French. In fact, it happened so often that Brad felt hostility from the other guys. He tried to tell them that he broke away as soon as he could, but they were not convinced. There was no farewell party when he left.

One strange requirement of the philosophy department at Berkeley for a Ph.D. was to have an MA in a different field. The reasoning behind this was that philosophy is so broad and all-embracing, you should have an MA in one of the arts to get a Ph.D. in aesthetics, or an MA in one of the physical sciences for a Ph.D. in metaphysics, etc. Students were convinced it was just to make it hard on them, and their only concern was what is the easiest route to an MA. Brad liked the requirement, as his love for literature grew daily. He decided on English poetry, with a thesis on the philosophical ideas contained in poems. Didn't someone say that poetry was the best thoughts of the best minds expressed in the best possible way?

When he registered in the department office, the secretary informed him he would have to show proficiency in a foreign language, but that he would have six months to take the test. Brad asked, "Can I take it now?"

"Now?" she replied.

"Yes, right now, here," he repeated. "My French will never be better than this very minute." So she got out the exam and he knocked it off.

The GI Bill was not quite enough to support him. He would have to work. Instead of straining his eyes still more with a library job, he looked for physical labor, thus getting exercise while earning money. He became a "bohunk." Bohunks load boxcars. There was a huge railroad yard in Oakland, a short ride from Berkeley. He worked with a wonderful assortment of uneducated men on the swing shift, four to twelve, so different from his daytime academics.

The foreman of Brad's eight-man crew was "Shorty." True, this fifty-year-old man was short, barely over five feet. But he had so many striking characteristics, it was a shame to settle for Shorty. This no-shouldered man wore pants too baggy and a leather jacket too tight, as ridiculous as Charlie Chaplin with none of the great comedian's charm. His Chaplin walk outdid Charlie's. His mouth contained no teeth. When he said, "We're gonna unload car seventeen on track five," no one understood him, but it didn't matter. They just followed him. One of the guys demonstrated his native tongue, Polish, and Curtis yelled, "Hey, Shorty, I just found out what language you speak!"

There was a lot of down time, waiting for a driver to pull up a string of dollies, into which they'd throw mail sacks bound for Fresno, Bartok, Bakersfield, San Mateo, Carmel. Now and then, the engineer would take them for a ride a few miles out and bring them back on a different track. It was a jolting ride, with stops that crammed the boxcars together. Slim, lying on a coffin, said, "Jesus, that goddam engineer gonna wake this dead man." Some guys played cards. Brad did not tell them he was writing poetry. Kidding was constant, sometimes vicious, mostly genial. A favorite trick was to appear to be struggling with a large, light box and, while handing it to the next guy, say, "Careful—heavy." That guy would almost throw it through the roof. The opposite also worked— nonchalantly, with one hand, pass a small heavy box and watch the next guy drop it.

Curtis was a huge, powerful man. No matter how fast he threw mail sacks, Shorty always yelled at him. Curtis would just grin and spit close to Shorty. Once Shorty got to him. Curtis walked over and stood with his chest inches from Shorty's nose. "Get off my back, Shorty! And stay off! Or I'm gonna drive you straight through this floor!"

Without conviction, Shorty said, "Tay office, tay office, tay office!" looking at the corner of the boxcar as if wishing Curtis were over there instead of at the end of his nose.

"Take me to the office! I'll go wicha! I'll go wicha!" screamed Curtis.

Shorty suddenly remembered he was needed somewhere else and hastened away, yelling, "Polack, move dolly, move dolly."

One of the crew, "Pigeon," often sneaked away, not to avoid work, but to care for his birds. The railroad yard was on the Bay, with several unused, rotting docks. Many pigeons nested there, and Pigeon harvested them. He performed dangerous acrobatics getting to the nests, and withstood dive-bombing attacks of shit. He plucked certain feathers from the baby birds so they could not fly. When they grew big enough, he took them home for dinner. He shared with the crew for covering him. Although he was married with four kids, Pigeon continually bragged about his bevy of girlfriends, especially his latest. One night after midnight, Brad was gassing up on his way home from work. Pigeon, who had the night off, pulled into the gas station. "Hey, Professor!" as they all called Brad, "Here's that hot stuff I told you about! Is she beautiful or what?"

Brad was leaning in the passenger window. "From what I can see, yes, she's very beautiful." To leave no doubt, she pulled her strapless top down to her waist.

Pigeon laughed loud with delight and started to pull away, shouting, "You two gonna get us arrested!" but Brad was already halfway in the window. Pigeon was laughing so hard he could hardly get the words out—"You one crazy dude, Professor! Lemme go!" They reached the end of the gas station and Brad reluctantly backed out. He could still hear Pigeon laughing as the car hit the highway.

Shorty, who never dated, who never even looked at women or talked about them, stunned everyone by announcing he had just got married. She was twenty years younger, a pennyless drifter, attractive in a sluttish sort of way. She saw a meal ticket and grabbed him. She broke his spirit. He no longer yelled at his crew, no longer seemed comical, only pathetic. She insisted on taking a vacation on a Mexican beach. Can you commit suicide by catching pneumonia? Shorty did.

Brad lived in a large house that had been turned into rooms for rent. His room was on the third floor. On the second floor lived Lorina, a very slender, very graceful black secretary. They sometimes met, coming and going. At first it was just a "hi." That gradually grew into a few minutes of light banter. About a week before the night Brad ran into Pigeon at the gas station, he and Lorina happened to enter the house together. She said, "I worked so hard today, I'm not sure I can make it up the stairs."

"Let me help you," said Brad, swooping her up and carrying her up the stairs.

Between giggles, she protested, "Oh please, put me down," without the slightest hint of meaning it. When they got to the second floor, Brad said, "I could easily carry you up another flight."

"No," she said warmly but firmly.

"Will you come up for a drink?" he asked.

"Yes," she answered, "but I'll walk."

He stood her on her feet and they went up to his room. He poured them some Dubonnet, turned on easy listening, and they exchanged life stories. Eventually, he said , "Let's dance." They did. He held her very close.

"This is more than dancing," she said.

"Yes," he agreed. "I just wanted an excuse to hold you."

She separated and said, "I enjoyed our happy hour, including the dance, but I want to leave now." She gave him a quick kiss and was gone.

A week later, he lay in bed, frustrated, thinking about Pigeon's beautiful girlfriend. It was 1:00 AM. There was a knock on his door. When he opened it, there stood Lorina, wearing a revealing nightgown. "I locked myself out. Can you help me get in?"

"What happened?" he asked. "Come in."

"No, please, just go down to the basement and get a key from the janitor."

"He won't give me the key to your room without your permission, and you don't want him to see us like this at one in the morning." He was wearing nothing but a towel. "What happened?" he asked again, gently escorting her into his room.

"Well," she began, "I was feeling so lonely, and I heard you come home, and I debated coming up. I stepped into the hall to see if anyone was around. The coast was clear, but I decided not to come. I turned to go back into my room, but I had locked myself out."

Holding her in his arms, he said, "Aphrodite had obviously decided you must come to me. Spend the night with me and we'll get your key in the morning." By the time he finished talking, he had already lowered her straps and was kissing her small, firm breasts. He was thrilled by her long nipples and wondered if she had nursed a baby, but this was hardly the time to ask. All of her skin was tight and smooth. In the morning, they could not remember when the hours of sex had stopped and sleep had begun, as they were still wrapped in each others' arms upon awakening. When he got home from work that night, there was a note under his door: "Last night was beautiful. I will always look back at it fondly as a very dear memory. But for many reasons, I don't want it to happen again. Thank you. God bless. Lorina." Despite living in the same house, he never saw her again.

Chapter XII

*B*RAD was taking a few philosophy courses toward his eventual Ph.D., but mostly English courses for his required master's. The trend in philosophy was to studiously avoid analogies, as your argument might use that aspect where the analogy breaks down to falsely prove a point. Brad, the poet, missed those vivid analogies of Plato, where people were chained in a cave and could only see their shadows on the wall, thinking the shadows were reality. These people were banned from knowing the beauty of sunlight which shined upon the real world and cast the shadows. When one broke loose and told the others about the real world, they thought him crazy. Brad loved that. But these contemporary philosophers wrote in turgid, paragraph-long sentences, inventing their own multi-syllabic terms. Thoroughly convinced schools of thought sneered at other thoroughly convinced schools. "Logical Positivists" sneered the most.

Brad felt more at home in poetry classes, where "one flash of Truth within the tavern caught, better than in the temple lost outright!" While he loaded boxcars, the arguments of the Logical Positivists were forced out by the wonderful words of poets: tiger, tiger, burning bright—O wild west wind—the shot heard round the world—where ignorant armies clash by night—twas brillig, and the slythy toad did gire and gimble in the wabe—Christ! What are patterns for?—something there is that does not love a wall—tell me if the lovers are the losers, if any get more in the dust, in the cool tombs.

Brad enthusiastically walked into the first class of "Contemporary Poetry," expecting to look deeper into those living poets he knew—Robert Frost, T.S. Eliot, Carl Sandburg, Ezra Pound, e.e. cummings, etc. Great poets had replaced his lost biblical prophets. Where once he lingered on the wisdom of "let he who is sinless cast the first stone," he now marveled at how perfectly great poets put the big truths—humans as "sole judge of truth, in endless error hurled; the glory, jest and riddle of the world." Once his joy was feeling "the kingdom of heaven is within you." Now his joie de vivre was "My heart leaps up when I behold a rainbow in the sky. So be it when I shall grow old, or LET ME DIE!" Not long ago, he had watched and heard Frost read his poetry. Likewise T.S. Eliot. He idolized them both. He yearned to be a "contemporary poet" and eagerly awaited encountering those who had officially acquired that title in this course.

The professor was young, dynamic and self-confident verging on arrogant. "I hope none of you think," he said with a sarcastic grin, "that because Frost and that crowd of old men are still alive, that they are contemporary poets. They were born in the 1800s and wrote closer to World War I than to our recent war. You know, history books show us pictures of great men as old men, trying to con us into worshiping our elders. But that Methuselah over in Princeton, with his wild white hair and baggy sweater and pipe, exuding wisdom—HE didn't give us $E = MC^2$. A young patent office clerk in his twenties gave us relativity. Poets too. Byron, Keats and Shelley were smart enough to die young. Dylan Thomas just died at thirty-nine, so there won't be any phony photos of him as an old man. OK then, let's pay our respects to Carl Sandburg, who is still hanging around, and move on to the real contemporary poets."

Brad was amazed and delighted. Obviously, the professor was right. Poets who wrote around WWI were not "contemporary"in the 1950s. His heart leaped up at the thought that he was about to find out who were the poets near his age and how and what they wrote. He did know Dylan Thomas' already famous "rage, rage against the dying of the light" and that he, too, "would not go gentle into that good night."

So he learned about the Black Mountain Poets, the Beats, the San Francisco Renaissance, the New York School—and was horrified. Brad had long been familiar with "free verse," and some of his own poems took that form. Although some free verse fitted Louise Untermeyer's derisive description as "shredded prose," the best had a true poetic rhythm to their chaotic lines. Now Brad stared at lines which had some poetic music, but had no decipherable meaning. Like this by one of the leaders of one of the above-mentioned schools:

> I being you, you being other,
> all others being no one,
>> still Sisyphus (strong!) swims
>> against (look out!) the blood stream
>> of (vengeful!) Zeus' veins.
> Tread not (no!) the fronds
>> and pinnae of moonwort.
> Closed forever to migrant me
>> the Moravian Gate.
> To Phitsanulok then,
>> beauty beneath thatched hats,
>>> rats in rancid rice
>>> scent of sandalwood,
>>> omni-crassitude,
>>> omni-lassitude.

111

Death by (no, yes, no!) stibine sniff
       if
carnassical carnage causes cark—
Weep, O mine eyes!
     death itself dies!
        Exeunt!

Brad raised his hand and asked, "I guess I can look up 'fronds and pinnae,' but how am I you?"

The professor let out a loud laugh, barely concealing his annoyance and contempt. "Well," he said, "I can see you're really going to get your money's worth from this course. I'm going to bring you all the way up to the middle of the twentieth century."

Brad asked, "Are you going to tell me how I'm you?"

"Look," the prof said, not laughing, "poetry has already done the comparing to a summer's day, the midnight ride of Paul Revere. We've burned the candles at both ends, and now we're freeing words to sing any way they want to. No straightjacket iambs, no limiting prosaic meaning. Would you ask Beethoven what bum-bum-bum-bum means?"

Brad answered, "Of course not, because notes don't have verbal meaning. But words do. Wild imagery can be wonderful, but you have to understand the image. There's a fundamental difference between strange sense and nonsense. If this poem is nonsense to me, a graduate student in literature, where does the poet expect to find readers?"

"With people who read with their ears, not their eyes. Let prose make sense. Poetry makes music. All art is emotion, not reason. We're in a wonderful revolution. Painters let their brushes fly with no intention of representing anything. Composers ignore the standard scales. And poets put words together however it feels right, traditions and academicians be damned."

Later in the course, the professor assigned the students to

each write a poem in the "contemporary style" which he had been teaching them. That weekend, Brad came up with two poems which he thought met the requirement:

> The face on the barroom free lunch counter
>
> Choice of soup or juice or
> a pair of appetizers or better to open.
> But shouldn't the "entree" be the opener?
> And if "hors d'oevre" means "out of work,"
> is that what they hand out to bread lines?
> Or are they on bread lines
> because they can't speak French?
> No frog's legs for you, bum!
> Choice of what?
> Dessert and coffee not included.

The 2nd poem was:

> I,
> bird glide against gentle wind,
> standing still on my wings
> in the sky,
> was for a moment the only
> non-motion in the universe, saw for the first
> time ever how all things move.

Then Brad added, "However, my real love and talent is writing aphoristic poetry in the tradition of Robert Frost," and he added the following poems:

> Little creatures like the night,
> dart about in darker light.
> Lion aren't afraid to yawn
> at the fire dance of dawn.

And:

> Brendan Behan was a bum,
> a drunk like Dylan Thomas.
> Before they drowned, the only thing
> they did was keep their promise.

And a sonnet:

> How many times can a vow be taken,
> how many times be respoken?
> Which time will the brittle syllables break on
> temptation and have to be swept up broken?
>
> None of the many times, of course.
> China cement or flour and water will do.
> Leave over night under constant force.
> Hope springs eternal at the sight of glue.
>
> How do vows spring? Do Phoenixes fly?
> Does the jigsaw puzzle put perfectly together
> convey even what the poor print did
> of Constable's sky? Do Phoenixes sing?
> Can these questions excuse me now
> from picking up the pieces of my vow?

And of course he added the "giggling girls" poem which he had recited to his old gang at the beach.

A few days later, the professor discussed some of the students' poems with the class. "And now," he said, "I want to read to you a funny and clever tour-de-force, where Brad not only has end rhymes, but every syllable in the whole damned poem rhymes:

Giggling girls with wiggling curls
were walking down the street.
Whistling guys with bristling thighs
were talking indiscreet.
Hacked, bland hags with black handbags
sneered that it was outrageous.
Eye-glassed men with bypassed yen
feared that it was contagious."

The class laughed. "Brad and all of you," the prof continued, "regular rhythm and rhyme are not taboo in contemporary poetry. Dylan Thomas' recent poem 'Do Not Go Gentle into that Good Night,' is good old iambic pentameter, and every triplet has the exact same rhyme scheme: ite, ay, ite. And anyone can understand every line. The point is that ninety-nine percent of the time, contemporary poets, including Thomas, feel choked and cramped by these restrictions. They want to put down whatever words sound right to them, even when they don't know why or what they mean."

Brad asked, "And isn't that the ninety-nine percent of the time they don't get read?"

"No," the prof answered, "that's the ninety-nine percent of the time when they are truly contemporary poets. Brad, you would have been a very good poet fifty years ago."

As the semester progressed, sadness overwhelmed Brad's natural gladness. He felt a three-fold loss. First, careful thought had ripped his naive religion from him. He had lost his great love of Jesus and the Bible. Second, philosophy was not opening the door to any ultimate truths, only exposing the fallacies of all schools of thought. And third, poets were killing poetry. Suddenly, only one thing seemed solid in his dissolving world—his love for Kay. As they had not exchanged letters for almost two months, he wanted to see, as he so often had, her delighted surprise when he showed up without alerting her. As soon as the semester ended, he would fly to her.

Chapter XIII

*B*RAD boarded the plane in San Francisco at 10:00 PM. With the six hours in the air, the three time zones and a layover, it was 10:00 AM before he drove the rented car out of Newark Airport, as we mentioned at the beginning of this story. He drove along the Jersey Turnpike seeing how fast he could go through the toll booths and still hit the baskets with quarters. He had not seen Kay since he returned from France, two years ago. On the long flight across the country, he concluded that he would not continue toward a Ph.D. in philosophy. No matter how much his poetry was rejected, he now knew for certain that he was, and would always be, a poet. With his master's degree in English, he would earn his keep as an English teacher, sharing other poets by day and being his own poet by night. Or maybe get a job as a night watchman and write all the time. He'd live in New York City or north Jersey, near Kay.

He drove along the familiar hometown streets which he so often had traveled on foot as a child, on roller skates as a boy, on a bicycle as a teen, on his motorcycle as a high school senior, and now much less intimately as a man in a car. He almost jammed on his brakes as he thought he saw Ed, but of course Ed was killed in the war. Passing through midtown, he stopped to stare at his old apartment building where, ten stories up, the acrobatic Jack Darin would jump onto the two-foot-wide edge and walk all the way around, while the terrified Brad watched. Brad drove up the hill toward Kay's, the hill which had always meant getting UP in the world. Hopefully, Kay would be reading in bed, wearing satin pajamas or a sheer nightgown. The daughter was away at school. Kay would undoubtedly be his alone.

He stepped out of the car and stood there, leaning on the door and looking over the car's roof at the path, the house, the grounds. All the times he had done so during these seventeen years raced through his memory like a movie run backwards, until he felt twelve again, about to meet Kay for the first time. The moment passed, and the grown-up man walked up to the house.

As he walked up the flagstone path, he knew he would not be intercepted by Kay's mother, as that worthy watchdog was now helping St. Peter guard the Gates. Kay answered the doorbell. Her tailored suit and hat startled Brad. Her smile was not the usual one of delighted surprise.

"Well," she said, "you're still good at unexpected entrances." Turning to the man standing behind her, "This young man is in the habit of disappearing for years, then suddenly popping up. Brad, this is Dr. Newman."

"New-man?" Brad asked.

"Yes," she replied, seeming to answer both questions.

"Hi," Brad said to this tall, handsome, greying forty-eight-year-old man who looked the perfect TV doctor.

"Pleased to meet you," replied the doctor, extending his hand. "We were just leaving for a quick lunch, as I have to be at the hospital at one. Would you care to join us?"

"No, thank you. I have so many other old friends to surprise."

Kay said, "I'll be home by 1:30. Call me."

Brad said he would and made a quick exit. For the first time, Brad wondered if Kay had had other affairs. If so, he certainly could not blame her, certainly not expect such a passionate woman to wait around a year or two for him to drop by. And he had had his flings. Actually, Kay had resisted many temptations for two reasons: First of all, she did not want to look in the mirror and see herself as a "loose woman." Secondly, she wanted to preserve the deep love and lust she felt for Brad. So from 11:30 to 1:30, he sat in the park and wrote:

> We held a ribbon, my love and I.
> We ran with it and watched it fly.
> O red, red ribbon, flying free,
> what has ever become of thee?

> We held a long ribbon, I and my love.
> The kind winds blew it way above
> and behind and beyond and around
> and somehow—it never touched the ground.

> A shiny ribbon, each held in a hand.
> That's all we had for a wedding band.
> "The links are heavy" she cried with pain.
> And sure enough, it became a chain.

> The cold steel dragged on the stones below.
> "There is no lock. You may let it go."
> She left it loose at the other end.
> I carry it now, like a crippled friend.

> O long red ribbon, shiny and free,
> what has ever become of thee?

At 1:30, he called. Kay said, "I don't want to talk on the phone, and I have to be a mother until 7:00. Can you meet me at The Olde Carriage House at 7:00?"

He agreed. Tears of hurt and anger and despair almost made him stumble as he wandered back to the park. He sat on the same bench and wrote:

> Other times I've lived without your love
> for half a day,
> half a moment when you looked away.
> But these minutes, these last few hours,
> I have not dared to live without your love.
> Even in the doubts of your eyes' silence,
> I dare not doubt.
> When I hung up our love just now in a phone booth,
> hung it up for 5 hours of not knowing,
> I felt for the first time I can remember
> the valuelessness of everything else.
> Even the great symbol of negotiability—
> I flung it—the change held
> in my hand to let me talk with you longer—
> I flung it into the street.
> And I flung from me the feeling of anyone near,
> walked and walked and crossed and recrossed
> the street not to pass a person. I wanted
> no one near if not you.
> When I had walked long enough to convince me
> my feet were still a part of me
> and I was still together,
> I came to this bench.
> I came to this bench to cry.
> The comfort of tears, the release,
> the rain falling on our hot sorrows,
> cooling and caressing the cheek,
> and I let the dark cloud in my heart burst.

I've never thought tears unmanly
and did not stop for that.
The practical side of love stopped me,
for I could not, even now after so much said
in so little on the phone, give you up.
I did not want you watching my puffy eyes. I,
in short, could not afford to cry.
I promised myself, if one day hence,
I had to face the void,
enough tears to water all my sorrows.
My finger-hanging hopes hung hopelessly
on looking my best.
I would wash my face
and become loveable in some new way,
Knowing there was nothing new to do
and nothing new would matter.

I have looked over the cliff before,
into the valley where you are not.
I fancied I felt the earth giving way,
yet knew quite truly they
were fears, not mountains being humbled.
Now it's more than fear.
I've heard the earth rumble.
I've seen the trees shake.
I've watched the hope crumble.
I've felt the heart break.
And still I tell myself
that it will be 5 hours till I know
if this will be a seismographic news item,
sticking no farther into my life
than a technological needle,
or whether I shall learn the news
looking up from our love's grave.
So I cannot afford,

as I have done before
when looking over,
to live with the despair.
Now it is too real.
I must make believe it is not there.
Make myself believe that
between now and then,
you will remember what our love has been,
remember what you think you do remember
but forgot.
I must pass the time without tears
and pretend you do not come to say goodbye.

At 7:00, Brad arrived at the pub. He sought the most secluded booth. Kay soon entered. He rose. She hugged him, but did not kiss him. They sat. He said, "Read this," and gave her the "red ribbon" poem.

Her eyes teared. She forced herself not to cry. "It's beautiful. You've come a long way from that schoolboy poem you gave me."

Brad said, "I've been writing all day. Read this," and put the other poem in front of her.

This time she could not help but cry. "Oh Brad, I've loved you as much as anyone can love. Many times you could have said 'come with me' and I would not have even asked where. I'm ashamed to admit I would have even abandoned my child. But I've finally grown up. I belong with someone my own age. You are about to change from a boy to a man, and you should be with someone your own age."

Brad protested, "But we've shared so much for so long!"

"Have we really? Every year or two, a few days. We've spent more time reading each others' letters than in each others' arms."

Brad pleaded, "That will change! I'm not going on for my doctorate. I'll get a teaching job here, near you. We'll see each other all the time!"

Kay shook her head. "I won't say I'm ending this for you, because I'm not. But I know it's better for you to build an adult life without me. The loving was exquisite, but it's over, and it should be."

Brad tried once more, "Can we visit or talk or write?"

"No," she insisted, "it was too thrilling to come down now to street level. Let's treasure the memories and let go."

He knew there was nothing more to say. She got up, gently touched his cheek and was gone.

On the drive back to Newark Airport, he refused to consider the possibility that Kay was right. It still hurt too much. A major part of his future plans, to be with Kay, had been ripped from him. However, it did not shake in the slightest his pledge to himself to be a poet. He remembered that someone had said that writers have no bad experiences— it's all material. Suddenly, in the middle of his sadness, a laugh burst out, as the old high school pun flashed into his mind, and he put together this doggerel:

> I've had me many a magic day,
> bedding a lovely maid.
> But tell her, please, if you see Kay,
> she was the best I've laid.

Printed in the United States
38833LVS00002B/91-141